City of the Dead
The Fascinating Supernatural History of Edinburgh

Jan-Andrew Henderson

A Black Hart Publication

Scotland. Australia

Jan-Andrew Henderson/Black Hart Publishing
32 Glen Coul Ave, Dalgetty Bay, Fife, Scotland KY11 9XL
6 Redgum Close, Bellbowrie, Qld, Australia 4070
www.cityofthedead.com

The rights of the author to be identified as the author of this work has been ascertained in accordance with the Copyrights, Designs and Patents Act 1988.

Book Layout © 2019 BookDesignTemplates.com

City of the Dead by Jan-Andrew Henderson
1st ed 2004 by Black and White Publishers.
Reprinted and updated 2019.by Black Hart

ISBN 978-0-9928561-3-7
ISBN 978-0-9928561-4-4 (Ebook)

For the City of the Dead's tour guides.

They keep us in touch with our past and bring it back to life

The character of a place is often most perfectly expressed in its associations... So, in the low dens and high-flying garrets of Edinburgh, people may go back upon dark passages in the town's adventures, and chill their marrow with winter's tales.

Robert Louis Stevenson

CONTENTS

Chapter 1

Introduction

Occult. Hidden from the eye or the understanding. Invisible. Secret. Concealed. Unknown.

Webster's Dictionary

I might seem an unlikely candidate to write a book about the supernatural.

All right, I've written one before and I know how lucrative spooky tales can be, but I don't actually believe in ghosts. I don't believe in astrology or UFO's or the Loch Ness Monster or the Devil. I've met secret societies, Satanists and witches - I've even been cursed by one. But I don't think they have any genuine powers.

Of course, I could be wrong.

But I *do* know Edinburgh, a modern, lively capital in a civilized western country - and southern Scots are pragmatic, practical and not particularly religious these days. Yet this city has the reputation for being the most haunted on earth.

That's the reason for this book.

It's a history of the dark side of Edinburgh, a city whose past is as black as the Earl of Hell's waistcoat. It's a guide book to all the grisly and supernatural locations in the capital. And it's a bit of an investigation – into the occult in general and Edinburgh's connections to it.

Just how *did* this city get such a sinister reputation? Is it all as insubstantial as a spectre? Or is there really something strange and supernatural going on?

Let's take a look.

Chapter 2

A Brief History of Edinburgh

*History is indeed little more than the register of the crimes, fol-
lies, and misfortunes of mankind*

Edward Gibbon

They came running down the Royal Mile.

*Women. Dozens of them. Sleeves rolled up round their scabby
arms. Panting like dogs. Dank, sweaty hair whipping across their faces. Ragged skirts gathered up over their thighs. Behind them surged
the Edinburgh mob, who had sensed something terrible or exciting
was about to happen and were hoping for both.*

*The women reached the nursery in twos and threes, the older or
more feeble ones beginning to stagger. They held on to each other for
support, red faces twisted with exhaustion and fear.*

*A crowd had gathered here as well, but they kept a wary distance
from the closed nursery door. A group of councillors huddled beside
the entrance, talking to the cleansers. All looked unsettled, casting
frequent nervous glances at the throng. The cleansers were wearing
conical masks filled with herbs and, at the sight, two of the women
collapsed.*

2 · JAN-ANDREW HENDERSON

A large female stepped forward. She was as tall and broad as any of the men and her burly arms were weathered like ship rope. Her fists clenched and unclenched.

"My name is Elspeth Dunrobbie," she shouted, pointing to the closed door. "And my lad is in there." She indicated the other terrified mothers. "All oor bairns are lodged here while we are at work. All oor children!"

A councillor took her arm.

"Some o the younger ones hae the sign," he said quietly.

Elspeth Dunrobbie clutched at her greasy hair and screwed both eyes shut. Behind, a sorrowful wail rose from her companions. She shook off the councillor's arm with a furious shrug.

"I want tae be with my son!"

"Do ye no understand woman? The plague has broken oot in there!"

Elspeth Dunrobbie took a deep, fluttering breath.

"I want tae be with my son," she repeated.

She stared into the councillor's eyes. The crowd tried to push forward and get a better look at this battle of wills. The official glanced at the throng with undisguised hatred. One or two of them held planks and axe handles.

He turned to the cleansers.

"Let her in."

Two of the masked men opened the nursery door. They could hear children crying somewhere inside.

Elspeth Dunrobbie took one last look at the sun, floating in the smoky air above the tenements. Then she ran to her son.

One by one the other women followed her. Some held hands. Others prayed. One or two wept. Most simply looked resigned, an expression that sat easily on the faces of those who had only ever known disappointment and toil.

When they were all inside the councillor nodded to the cleansers.

"Brick up the doorway."

There was an angry roar from the mob, now twenty persons deep. The ring of threatening humanity began to close in on the officials.

"What!" the councillor cried. "You want tae let them come oot again? Aye, and their pox ridden brats wi them? You want the plague spread among you faster than a horse can gallop?"

No one met his eye. The councillor waved his hand indicating that the cleansers were to continue.

"Brick the nursery door up!" he insisted.

And so they did

The nursery is long gone but Edinburgh's Museum of Childhood is said to be built on the site. And, of course, the area is reputed to be haunted by the voices of crying children. Small wonder really, with all those toys sitting around and no way to play with them.

The plague in the nursery is one of the countless gory legends about Edinburgh's past and one of the many of ghost stories associated with the city - the two are usually connected. After all, the best tales always involve dirty deeds and dreadful deaths, which may go a long way to explaining why Edinburgh seems to have so many restless spirits.

This is a book about the occult and supernatural elements of the city but, before we get to that, it's best to know what sort of place we're talking about. And the best way to do that is to give a brief account of the history of Edinburgh.

If you want to go straight to the supernatural stuff, you can miss it out. But when I start talking about Covenanters or the Battle of Flodden later on, and you haven't a clue what they are, you've only got yourself to blame.

Most visitors agree the capital is a lovely place. They marvel at the beautiful architecture, stroll through landscaped parks, gasp at the cost of the Scottish Parliament Building and laugh at its funny shape. They enjoy the city's cosmopolitan atmosphere, party at its festivals and celebrate its late opening pubs. Actually, they get steaming drunk in its late opening pubs, which probably explains *some* of the ghost stories.

Edinburgh's urbane splendour hints at a fine, elegant, cultured history. All right, there's been the odd massacre or two, but even the most civilized capitals have a couple of skeletons in their historical closet. So surely Edinburgh is no exception.

Well, actually this city *is* an exception

This city has enough skeletons in its closet to take out and fill a graveyard.

* * * *

To be honest, life in ancient Edinburgh seems to have been fairly similar to the rest of Europe. The castle provided protection for two rows of houses running along the Old Town ridge – the street which is now known as the Royal Mile. Crops were grown on partitioned 'enclosures' which sloped down from the ridge to flat pastureland on either side of the settlement. Apart from constant wind, rain, midges, disease and two brutal English occupations between 1174 and 1341, it all sounds rather pleasant. The writer Froissart, visiting Edinburgh in 1384 called it the *Paris of Scotland* and it seems to have remained a bustling but agreeable place until the 15th century. Well, as agreeable as a medieval town with no sanitation, medicine or running water can get.

Around this time Robert II came to power, the first of 14 Stuart kings. From then on the fate of this dynasty would be inextricably linked with that of the city – and it wasn't a good thing for either.

Robert II and Robert III set the pattern for this love/hate relationship between Scotland's capital and its monarchs. Both were feeble rulers and allowed the southern Scots nobles to pretty much do what they liked, which was generally bleed their own peasants dry then invade England. This brutal aristocracy soon got *used* to doing what they liked and the result was centuries of bloodshed – with Edinburgh at the centre.

The next Stuart ruler, James I, suffered the consequences of his father's shaky reign. To escape the unruly nobles Robert III sent his son to France for safety - and then promptly died. Unfortunately James was captured en route by the English and held to ransom. After 17 years it became apparent that nobody in Scotland was ever going to pay to get their king back, so the English let him go.

He returned to Edinburgh in 1420, an angry man in a hurry to rule his country. The nobles weren't going to put up with *that* kind of interference and eventually murdered him.

And so James II came to power at 6 years old, a pawn of his own upper class relatives. In one famous incident they persuaded the boy king to arrest and execute the 16 year old Earl of Douglas and his younger brother at a dinner party in the castle – a shocking breach of culinary etiquette.

But things really started going wrong for Edinburgh when the Scots got into yet another tiff with their southern neighbours.

In 1450 James II defeated the English at the Battle of Sark. This came as rather a surprise to the Scots – losing battles was almost their national sport. The king, quite naturally, feared an English reprisal and, by the law of averages, the Scots weren't due to win another fight against their 'Auld Enemy' for several centuries. He ordered a defensive wall to be built round the capital and the north pastures were flooded to impede would be attackers – a huge swamp which became known as the 'Nor Loch'.

James didn't live to see if his wall worked. While trying to put down another aristocratic uprising he was blown up by one of his own cannon. Typical Stuart luck, really.

James III came to power at 9 and, deeply unpopular, struggled to keep his throne. Fighting his own peers, he fell from his horse and was carried to a nearby mill. In case his wounds were serious he asked to confess to a priest. The miller's wife ran out to get one, but managed to bring back an assassin. That's country folk for you.

Edinburgh's new defences, in the meantime, became a double edged sword. The wall wasn't much use at preventing attacks but it did help stop the expansion of a capital city whose population was steadily growing. In 1500, Protocol books show the ground within the wall rapidly becoming covered by tall buildings. These were the 'lands' or 'tenements' – in effect the world's first skyscrapers – reaching an astonishing 15 stories in some places. Life was starting to get very cramped in the city.

And it was soon about to get a lot worse.

James IV was charming, strong and intelligent and under his rule Edinburgh seemed set began to flourish at last. Typically, he threw it all away, helping the French in yet another pointless war against the English. In 1513 he left Edinburgh with the greatest army Scotland had ever produced and invaded the south. They met a tiny English army at Flodden and the English wiped them out.

This was an even worse military move then beating the Auld Enemy! Knowing they had left themselves wide open to counter attack, the people of Edinburgh frantically began building a much larger defence - the Flodden Wall. It was a magnificent structure, ringing the whole city in an impenetrable casing of stone, so it's a bit of a shame the English didn't actually turn up to fight.

Then again, they didn't have to. The citizens had just made life worse for themselves than an enemy invasion ever could.

Trapped behind the Flodden wall the growing populace reached ridiculous levels of overcrowding. Rich and poor lived shoulder to shoulder in claustrophobic squalor. Dwellings began to pile up haphazardly over each other and the green enclosures vanished – nothing left but narrow passages between towering structures. Out of space and unable to erect edifices any higher, city builders began to dig into the ground. An Underground City was born – with thousands of people living in cellars, tunnels and chambers in unimaginable poverty.

As if this state of affairs wasn't nasty enough, Edinburgh had no sewage system to get rid of its masses of filth. The method of garbage disposal in the Old Town was to shout 'Gardy-loo' and throw everything out the window. (Gardy-loo was a warped version of *regardez de l'eau*, French for 'watch out for the water'). Except it wasn't water the warning referred to.

Household rubbish, the contents of chamber pots, that dead rat you found behind the door – everything went out the window. The waste became so thick that residents had to cut channels through solid rubbish to get to their front doors. Effluence drained into the narrow closes sloping down from the High Street Ridge until it was ankle deep. It seeped into the subterranean chambers of the Underground City and turned the nearby Nor Loch into a stinking, fetid sewer.

These were the social, economic and topographical conditions in Edinburgh from the 15th century up until the end of the 18th century. During that time, it was the most overcrowded city in Europe as well as one of the most unsanitary, violent and poverty stricken. Disease was endemic and frequent plagues ravaged a population living in such close and unhygienic conditions. It's hard to imagine how insanely overcrowded Edinburgh would have become if everyone had stayed healthy.

And in the middle of this muck and misery a religious conflict was brewing that would tear the city apart.

The Reformation in Europe had seen the rise of various forms of Protestantism. Persecuted by the Catholic Church in their own countries, many of these 'Reformers' fled to Edinburgh. Not that it helped them much, as they were persecuted here too.

But the movement grew in strength and the fight for the faith of the city's population was on with a vengeance – both sides ignoring the fact that the citizens needed a bath and a sandwich more than they needed a theological battle.

And that war was being settled by weapons rather than words.

A perfect example is the 'Cleansing of the Causeway'. In 1520, two of Edinburgh's major families – the Hamiltons and the Douglas's - took part in Scotland's biggest street fight and their supporters fought a running battle through the city that resulted in an alleged 300 fatalities

The Hamilton leader was James Hamilton of Finnairt (Catholic) – assisted by Cardinal James Beaton (ditto). In 1526 Finnairt murdered The Earl of Lennox (Protestant). The Earl's son (Protestant) then murdered Finnairt's brother, John Hamilton - the archbishop of St Andrews (Catholic, obviously). In 1528 Beaton and Finnairt played a prominent part in bringing Finnairt's cousin, Patrick Hamilton, to the stake for (Protestant) heresies. Cardinal Beaton appointed his nephew David a (Catholic) Cardinal. David was then murdered by Protestant reformers. Patrick's brother revealed to James V a plot to murder the king in which Finnairt was alleged to be involved. James was a Catholic but he wasn't stupid and had him killed anyway.

See what I mean?

The Stuart kings were still having their monumental run of bad luck. James V had become ruler at 17 months and was kept a virtual prisoner by his own nobles until he escaped at 17 years. Like his father he aided the French by sending a huge army against a tiny English force and, again, the Scots were sent packing at the battle of Solway Moss. This defeat wrecked the king's health and he died the same week as his heir was born. Mary Queen of Scots became queen at 6 days old.

This event was watched carefully by Henry VIII of England – who could see an opportunity to destroy Scotland's annoying alliance with the French by marrying Mary to his own son. When Mary's mother declined the offer, Henry began the 'Rough Wooing'- marching north and burning Edinburgh to the ground. Mary was sent to France for safety and didn't return until she was 19.

She came back to a city that was rougher than a Mexican border town on pay-day. Religious reform had gripped Edinburgh and the fiery preacher John Knox railed against Catholics, women and Mary Queen of Scots – who had the misfortune to be all three. Witch burning was common and torture was regularly used to get confessions out of anyone unlucky enough to be arrested.

Mary's return re-ignited the violence between the Catholics and the reformed 'Presbyterian' Protestants. Events spun out of her control and she finally fled south. In a history of dubious decision by Mary, making this move took the biscuit. Fearing that the Scot's queen (who had a decent claim to be her cousin Elizabeth's heir) would become a figurehead for the Catholic cause in England, Elizabeth I imprisoned her for 19 years, then executed her.

When Elizabeth died childless, Mary's son, James VI, suddenly found himself King of Britain. The Scots were ecstatic. After hundreds of years of trying to invade their old adversary, England had been handed to them on a plate!

James saw things a little differently. He promptly left Edinburgh, relocated to London and only came back once. Presumably to collect his stuff

But Edinburgh wasn't going to let the Stuarts go *that* easily.

While James settled down and Anglified himself, an even larger religious feud was brewing up north – one in which Edinburgh would again take a central role. Once again the consequences would be disastrous for the city.

By 1560 the Catholics were in the minority and the Presbyterians had become utterly fanatical about their religion. Scotland was dirt poor. Nothing grew here. It rained all the time. The highlands were a no go area filled with hairy men in plaid. The capital of the country was a hellhole. Even their king hated them.

Since they were not a world player in any other department, the Scots elevated their church to dizzy heights. They began to believe that they, and they alone, had a special covenant with God – that they were the real 'Chosen People'. Considering what traditionally happened to 'Chosen People', they might have thought this through a little more.

England on the other hand had a more relaxed form of Protestantism in the form of 'Episcopalianism'. This was basically a reformed version of the Catholic Church, with the king replacing the Pope as its head. It even had bishops.

The Scots didn't like that idea at all.

James VI, (now James I of Britain) had a go at dampening the Scot's religious fervour by introducing Episcopalianism into Edinburgh – and was quickly forced into a U turn when threatened with rebellion.

His son, Charles I, had no such qualms. Unlike his father he made no secret of the fact that he was Catholic. He couldn't force *that* on anybody - the English barely tolerated a Catholic on the throne as it was. But Episcopalianism was closer to Catholicism than Presbyterianism and he was determined it was going to be the religion of Scotland.

The conflict came to a head in 1637, when Charles ordered an Episcopalian prayer book be read out in Edinburgh's St Giles' Cathedral. A riot ensued which quickly escalated into a rebellion. Edinburgh's Presbyterians drew up a mission statement for their movement called the 'National Covenant'. The 'Covenanters' would remain loyal to Charles only if he stopped trying to mess with their religion. If he didn't there would be a holy war.

On 8th December 1638 the National Covent was signed in Greyfriars Church, Edinburgh, and, by the end of the year, with the exception of the Catholic stronghold that was the highlands, Scotland was fully and openly Presbyterian. Characteristically, Charles refused to back down and the 'Bishops Wars' began between the Covenanters and the Royalists.

But the overbearing king had little sympathy in England and the English 'Parliamentarians' also rose up against the despotic monarch. The English Civil War had begun. Charles was eventually defeated and, in 1650, Oliver Cromwell and the English Parliament executed the captured monarch.

The Scots were horrified! Despite a treaty with Cromwell and years spent fighting the tyrannical monarch, even the staunchest Covenanter took this as a national affront. The Stuarts were the line of Scots kings and the English couldn't just go around chopping their heads off. In Edinburgh's Parliament Square, the Covenanter leader, Argyll, proclaimed Charles' son the new ruler of Britain.

Mind you, the Covenanters didn't want him turning out like his father. They kept the young Charles II a virtual prisoner, while they moulded him into a good Protestant. The Stuarts were used to that by now but Charles certainly didn't appreciate it.

Cromwell retaliated by invading and occupying Edinburgh, forcing the new monarch into nine years of exile and destroying much of the Covenanter's power. But he proved to be as tyrannical as he was puritanical. When he died, both Scotland and England, suffering from terminal dullness, were happy to re-establish the monarchy.

Charles II was determined to never be a pawn again and crushed the Presbyterian movement in Scotland. He had Argyll executed outside St Giles Cathedral and set about annihilating what was left of the Covenanters.

They made their last stand at the battle of Bothwell Brig and were soundly defeated. Twelve hundred survivors were herded into Greyfriars Churchyard and locked in the northwest section (now known as the Covenanters Prison) – in effect the world's first concentration camp. The survivors were finally shipped to the West Indies to be sold as slaves but the ship sank and they all drowned.

It seems they weren't the chosen people after all.

In 1689 James II, last of the Stuart Kings was deposed (because he was Catholic, of course). James Graham of Claverhouse or 'Bonny Dundee' rode through the streets of Edinburgh shouting to the people to follow James's cause – and the fighting started all over again.

Famously, it was the highlanders who rallied to the Jacobite cause. Edinburgh citizens still didn't want to support an exiled Catholic king and, besides, they were tired of being the poorest and most dismal capital in Europe. Instead they poured their energies into a project they hoped would make Scotland a rival to the other great powers of the world.

The 'Darien Scheme' was the most ambitious colonial endeavour attempted in the 17th century. The brainchild of William Paterson – the Scot who founded the Bank of England – the idea was to command the trade of the Pacific and Atlantic by building a settlement on the Isthmus of Darien (the narrow neck of land separating North and South America, now known as Panama). England was naturally opposed to this new competition but the Scots didn't care. They jumped at the chance to be sole investors in their own fate and invested an astonishing half of the national capital in the project. Almost every Scot who had £5 to spare invested in the Darien Scheme and thousands more volunteered to travel on board the three fleets of ships that had been chartered to carry the pioneers to their new home.

It was a disaster.

Darien turned out to be an uninhabitable, mosquito-infested dump. The settlement was wiped out and only one ship made it back.

The Scottish economy was ruined – so much so that the Scottish Parliament agreed to join with the English one in exchange for aid. The citizens of Edinburgh rioted in the streets, as they always did when things went amiss, but it was no good. In 1707 the Scottish Parliament was dissolved and the country was joined with England.

You might think that union with a larger, richer, more stable nation would make Edinburgh a calmer place. Not at all. The Jacobites rebelled again in 1715 and swept south but were defeated just before they reached Edinburgh. Inside the city, nothing had improved. The famous 'Edinburgh Mob' rioted at the drop of a hat. In 1736 they famously dragged Captain John Porteus of the city guard from his cell (he was on trial for ordering his men to open fire on another riot) and hanged him in the street.

The police force was the laughable 'Old Town Guard'. They were composed mainly of ancient highlanders dressed in a dingy red uniforms and, according to contemporary writers, were 'an unfailing subject of mirth to the citizens of Edinburgh'. They were completely unable to deal with the city's crime wave – not really surprising, since it seemed to have lasted for centuries. Nevertheless, the Guard were not disbanded until 1817.

Then in 1745 the Jacobites were back and, this time, the rebellion was led by Bonnie Prince Charlie. He succeeded in capturing and occupying the city, but it was the last time Edinburgh would be invaded. A year later they were defeated at Culloden, the last battle fought on British soil, and the Jacobite cause ended forever.

Things were finally looking up for Edinburgh. For the first time the city actually seemed safe from invasion, so the council allowed the Flodden wall to crumble and the population to finally expand away from the Old Town ridge. By the end of the 18th century Edinburgh was undergoing an astonishing renaissance. The Nor Loch was drained. A magnificent New Town was built. The most learned men in the world gathered in the metropolis and Edinburgh became the official heart of the 'Scottish Enlightenment'. The city went from being a squalid little backwater to fame as the 'Athens of the North.'

Fantastic. Except everybody who was anybody had suddenly moved to the New Town. And into this vacuum poured a new population, turning the Old Town into an instant slum.

They came from the highlands, where the 'clearances' had emptied the land of Jacobites and replaced them with sheep. They came from the country, where the agricultural revolution was replacing the workers with machines. Most of all they came from Ireland where the potato famine was simply killing everybody.

Between the years 1800 and 1830, the population of Edinburgh doubled. While Edinburgh's luminaries in the New Town went about changing the world, the Old Town descended into a quagmire of violence, poverty, overcrowding and crime. It was as bad as it had ever been.

If anything, life was now harder for the citizens. Women working in the Lothian mines became deformed by the weights they had to carry. So did the children sent up narrow chimneys to sweep them. Whole families worked from dawn till late at night in airless, sweaty factories.

This population soon realised that the only way out of this poverty trap was to lie, cheat and steal their way to the top – and a criminal fraternity sprang up that would put the Mafia to shame.

These conditions bred some of Edinburgh's most famous villains, like the murderers Burke and Hare and the thief Deacon Brodie. They defined the character of Edinburgh the way strong spices flavour bad meat.

The situation took a long time to improve. In 1880, for instance, a typical tenement flat in the Old Town held the lodging house keeper, his family, eleven Bavarian musicians, eight Italian musicians and two shop keepers. It wasn't until the end of the 19th century that the worst of the slums were pulled down and proper reforms stilled the area's criminal heart.

Times have certainly changed. We've had a century of being a pretty nice place and the Royal Mile is now one of the world's top tourist destinations. But our real legacy is that, for half a millennium, we were the most badass capital on the planet.

Edinburgh's longtime rival, Glasgow, has a phrase that sums up this city perfectly. "All fur coat and no knickers."

How well they know us.

And *that's* the story of Edinburgh.

* * * *

A gruesome and violent history, however, isn't the same as a supernatural one. Plenty of places have had a shady past without invoking a haunted reputation. Edinburgh, on the other hand, seems to have more spectres and strange goings on than you can wave a scythe at. At the end of the book there is a comprehensive list of all the ghosts I could find reported in and around the city throughout its history.

But rather than just recycle the most unpleasant events in Edinburgh's past or rehash a bunch of ghostly tales - this book is a bit of a detective story. I'd like to try and discover what gives this city such a mysterious aura.

Our supernatural lore covers a lot more than a few wailing apparitions wandering around the grounds of deserted mansions. The city carries an air of mystery. The sense that there is a dark heart underneath a thin coating of civilisation. It has connections with Paganism, witchcraft, the occult, magic, Satanism, secret societies and a host of other mendacious associations. Some call it the *Jekyll and Hyde* city.

So, let's see if it's true.

This isn't just an exploration of darkest Edinburgh. It's also an investigation into the occult in general and all the creepy things people aren't sure about. Once we are clear what we are dealing with, we can see how Edinburgh, in particular, has come to be associated with them.

So how do we begin tying the history of the city to the history of the supernatural? The obvious way is to start at the beginning. Go back as far as we can and see where it leads us.

Let's start with the Pagans.

Chapter 3

Paganism

Scratch the Christian and you find the Pagan - spoiled.

Israel Zangwill

Darkness fell over Calton Hill.

A spring breeze ruffled the long grass and shadows slowly thick-ened, turning the huge hilltop to molasses. The blackness was punctuated with the moonlit outlines of an excited gathering – the main body clustered around the crown of the hill, and smaller groups thinning out over the slopes. The sound of drumming was drawing closer. Not one drum, not a dozen, but the pounding, surging, living rhythm that only massed percussion can make.

Over the brow of the hill came the Blue Men – the Druids – their bodies painted the colour of the sky, swaying in time to the rhythm. In the centre of their group was the May Queen, symbol of the earth. In stark contrast to her bright bodyguards, the woman's face was paint-ed chalk white, and she wore an ornate feathered headdress and embroidered robes. She looked down on a myriad of pinpoint lights floating on the sea of night that lapped the hill. Behind her, a set of giant stone pillars crawled with watchers. They clung on to any hand-holds their fingers could find, climbing as high as they could so they could see the spectacle better.

17

Silence fell over the watchers as the May Queen drew closer. At her side cavorted the Green Man, tall and slim and draped in shabby winter garments, bending and bowing around her like a Willow in the tempest of sound. From the four corners of the hill, Sylphs, Goblins, Nymphs and Sprites emerged hesitantly from the darkness. Startled, the crowd backed out of their way, letting the prancing creatures through to swell the numbers of their procession.

As the pageant completed the circle of the hill, the May Queen was ambushed.

From thick gorse bushes lining the path, the Red Men sprang forward. Naked and screaming, they rushed towards the procession, followed by their own furious drummers, stamping and shaking their heads in abandon. The pulsing rhythms merged with the existing beats and both rose to a crescendo. The Red men's gestures were lewd and their Devilish faces contorted as they writhed and cursed and tempted.

But the Blue Men held their ground around the May Queen, allowing her to carry on, unmolested, to the brow of the hill. She stared straight ahead, her face impassive, but her consort was overcome by the seductiveness of the moment. In a frenzy of passion the Green Man leaped for his mistress. He was dragged off and flung to the ground by her handmaidens, where he writhed orgiastically in the mud.

Many of the crowd had now begun to dance, caught up by the immediacy of this chaos. Some moved awkwardly at first, as those who dance from custom, but gradually they began to respond to the passion of the ceremony, to abandon themselves to its power. The Green man sprang to his feet, now stripped of winter garments. His lithe body, without the ragged trappings was young and strong.

A great fire sprang to life at the centre of the hill and the May Queen finally gave herself to the dance – merging with her emerald suitor in a marriage of music, heralding in a new summer. The entire procession twisted and swayed around the raging fire. The crowd were stamping and shaking their heads. Some of them howled at the sky just to hear the noise. The May procession began to slowly wind back down the hill.

Camera flashlights burst and faded around them like fireflies.

One of the Red Men strolled over to me. Only it was a woman.

"Got a cigarette?" she asked.

I fished one out of my pack and lit it for her. She didn't seem to be wearing anything but red paint, so I guessed she wouldn't have matches. Two elderly American tourists standing next to me were trying not to stare. The Red Woman winked and flounced off. The Americans gawped after her. I noticed that both were sweating profusely, despite the cold.

The woman patted her husband's arm.

"We haven't danced like that in years," she grinned.

Edinburgh's Beltane Fire Festival is arguably the largest Pagan ritual in the world – drawing an attendance of thousands every year. Yet, forty years ago Paganism was seen as an excuse for individuals of dubious morals and hair length to have sex in suburban living rooms.

Now it's the fastest growing religion in Scotland and Edinburgh is one of the world's largest Pagan centres.

To many people, however, Paganism still has a sinister air. Druids, witchcraft, standing stones, Lord of the Rings, pentagles and H P Lovecraft have got entangled in a mish-mash of legends about an ancient religion, obscured by the mists of time. The lingering perception is that there is something not quite right about the whole thing. And Scotland, where the old ways clung on longer than anywhere else, is particularly associated with this dark image. Just watch the film *The Wicker Man* for proof of that. Not the Nicholas cage remake, though. That's rubbish.

This bad reputation, it turns out, is largely manufactured. When Christianity swept across Europe, Paganism was its main victim. What the church couldn't incorporate, it demonized - and that air of suspicion remains today. Human beings, after all, have a tendency to accept what is drummed into them rather than go to the effort of finding out the facts.

So what are the facts? What is Paganism? Is the suspicion it engenders just because of bad press or does it really have a dark heart?

A heart that beats very strongly in Edinburgh.

Paganism may well be the world's oldest religion. As such it was suitably simple and functional – it had a hunter God and a fertility Goddess. Fair enough, since they represented the two most exciting things in prehistoric life.

Life operated in cycles and was itself a cycle – we came from mother earth and will return to it. All the objects around us are parts of this life force and, as such, are worthy of our respect.

Nothing very threatening in all that and the early Christians acknowledged this. In fact the term Pagan is derived from the Latin *Paganus*, which simply means country dweller – the people who held onto the old ways longest. And, though they banned Paganism as a religion, Christians were not above adopting its rituals, festivals and ideas to help convert its more stubborn adherents.

Christmas is a perfect example of this. In ancient Babylon, the 25th of December was known as 'Yule Day' or the promised child day – when the incarnate sun appeared as a baby child to redeem a world bound in darkness.

Sounds a bit familiar, doesn't it?

Yet it was not until centuries later, the latter part of the fourth century, that the Roman Christian Church began observing December 25th as Christ's birthday. They did so, knowing full well that other Pagan cults throughout Europe already celebrated the sun god, Mithra, on this selfsame day. This festival of Saturnalia was characterized by gift giving, coloured lights, festive meals, and of course, decorated trees. Not much to change then, which was handy for the Christians

As doctrines hardened, the fact that Christianity had adopted so many Pagan rituals and dates became a source of embarrassment to its more fervent believers. The famed Edinburgh preacher, John Knox, railed against the celebration of Christmas and Easter and the Church of Scotland eventually banned them as holidays. It was not until the turn of the 19th century that various yuletide customs began reappearing in Scottish Presbyterian churches and, as late as 1962, the Synod of the Free Presbyterian Church of Scotland stated that they *still* rejected these celebrations.

What the early Roman Catholic Church couldn't hijack it vilified. Since Paganism was older, well entrenched and a hell of a lot more fun, it bore the full brunt of Christian zeal. It was condemned as an ancient evil to be rooted out. The horned God of hunting was equated with the Devil, sex became a dirty word and nobody talked to the trees anymore.

Today we still live with this legacy. The Pagan pentangle is regarded as a symbol of evil, scrawled in blood on the walls of a thousand horror movies. In fact it is simply the symbol of the feminine side of nature, nothing more. Even the word for the superstitious country folk, those who clung longest to nature worship, was perverted. *Villanus* the old Latin name for field hand, became 'villain'.

Did the Pagans indulge in any kind of perverse or violent practices, something that might have lingered on in Scotland longer than anywhere else? In fact, there's no solid evidence that they practised human sacrifice or indulged in any particularly sordid rituals. Though Edinburgh is now the capital of modern Paganism, there is no evidence that its present day adherents are anything but nature lovers with a lot of pierced body parts and an aversion to washing their hair. As Professor Ronald Hutton of the University of Bristol succinctly put it

"Traditional religions have so many prohibitions: Thou shalt not do this or that. But Paganism has a message of liberation combined with good citizenship."

But old perceptions die hard and Edinburgh's strong Pagan connections have helped cement its dark image. Rather unfair when you remember that the Christians tortured and sacrificed thousands to *their* differing versions of God – an orgy of persecution that Edinburgh once happily participated in.

And this chapter in its history, quite rightly, coloured the city a darker shade.

For it led to the witch burning times.

Chapter 4

Witchcraft

There are three classes into which all the women past seventy that ever I knew were to be divided: 1. That dear old soul. 2. That old woman. 3. That old witch.

Marcus Aurelius

It was early morning, not long after dawn, and the smoke from dozens of cooking fires had fused with the morning mist over the Nor Loch. The smelly pall obscured the jagged tenements of the Old Town and even the wooden ramparts of Edinburgh castle drifted in and out of existence, as if part of some shabby fairy tale.

Along the soiled black banks of the Loch a crowd of several hundred had gathered. Some whispered. Some joked. Some looked frightened. Many appeared angry. All were tense with anticipation. The more enterprising had erected makeshift vantage points out of broken salt barrels and waterlogged ballast sacks and were charging a small fee for their use.

At six o clock the gates of the castle swung open and a dozen soldiers escorted a lone woman down the steep side of Old Town Ridge towards the gathering. In front of them strode the town Magistrate and the Minister of St Giles' Cathedral.

The haar had cleared and, as the prisoner approached, it became obvious that this was a lady of some bearing. She held herself erect, looking neither left nor right. She had been given a grey shapeless shift to wear but her pretty face was delicate and clean and her long auburn hair combed.

At the edge of the Nor Loch the Minister and the Magistrate, both dressed in black, climbed onto a rickety platform ringed by a waist high railing. The Magistrate read out the charges from a roll of parchment.

"Eufame McCalzean," he proclaimed. "In this year of our Lord 1592, and under the witness of God and the courts, you stand accused of practising the art of Witchcraft. It is alleged by several parties, that your abominable acts do include the casting of spells and the making of waxen pictures to be enchanted."

The woman gave a snort of derision. The Minister glowered at her. The Magistrate paused to raise a stately eyebrow then began to read again.

"It is also alleged that you did conspire with the Devil to do harm to that great personage, His Majesty King James VI."

There was an excited babble from the gathered crowd. In a city the size of Edinburgh, there wasn't a soul who didn't already know the charge, but hearing it read out seemed to make the crime even more hideous. An attempt on the life of the King!

The Magistrate eventually held up his hand for silence.

"With other sisters of your coven," he continued. "It is alleged that you did dance naked with Satan and use black arts to raise a great tempest off the coast of North Berwick. This storm was intended to bring devastation on the fleet and personage of his Royal Majesty King James, returning by sea with his new bride, Anne of Denmark."

In the middle of the crowd a small group, wrapped in heavy cloaks with the hoods raised, inched closer to the edge of the loch at the point where the throng was thinnest. Only the braver souls stood close to the water. For a century the effluence from the cramped and crowded Old Town had flowed down the hill and into the dark abyss. Now it stank like a rotting corpse and a ring of thick yellow foam marked its boundary.

"What reason have I to harm my King?" the woman spoke loudly. "And what do I know of storms or the sea?" Eufame McCalzean glanced at the thick dirty water and a note of panic crept into her voice. "I cannot even swim."

"Silence!" the Minister roared. "You made light enough of these charges when they were first brought."

"I did not think them serious!" the woman pleaded. "I am of a good family. Anyone who knows me understands these accusations are false."

She looked at the crowd for support and there were many who turned away rather than meet her eyes. Then again there were those who smiled and jabbered, excited at the prospect of what was to come. Whether Eufame McCalzean was guilty or not hardly mattered to them.

It does not necessarily take a minion of Satan to bring out the evil in men.

"Praise be to the Lord Almighty, whose protection of the saintly James kept him from drowning," said the Magistrate. "On his order you are to be dooked in the Nor Loch as a test of your own goodliness. Should you float, it will be a sign that you are indeed a witch."

"God bless the King," added the Minister and the crowd automatically repeated the mantra.

The Magistrate waved his arm and two soldiers stepped forward, seized the woman and forced her to her knees. With a hand on the back of her head, one burly guard pushed her face down into the mud and she turned her head just in time to avoid a mouthful of the stinking muck. The other knelt on her arched back, roughly tied her wrists together, looped the rope round her ankles and fastened it tight. Two longer ropes were then threaded through the gap, a simple apparatus to pull the woman back out of the water, should she start to drown.

For the first time, Eufame McCalzean seemed to realize how serious her situation was. As the soldiers picked her up she began to thrash her head from side to side trying to unbalance them. One slipped and went down on his knees and a quickly stifled burst of laughter rose from the crowd. The soldier cursed and slammed his gloved fist into the woman's face, breaking her nose and splitting her lips. The two men then waded into the filthy loch, dragging her between them, until the grey water reached the top of their thighs and poured over the rims of their riding boots. Waves lapped at the girl's blood covered mouth, spreading and thinning a red wash across her face, restoring her to consciousness. The soldiers looked at each other and began to count. With a practised gait they swung the screaming woman back and forwards, as if preparing to hurl a sandbag onto a barricade.

Eufame's wail rose in pitch as they let her go, then was cut sharply off as she plunged into the water several feet further out. The soldiers retreated back from the splash and the crowd held its breath.

At first there were only sluggish, widening ripples to show where Eufame McCalzean had vanished. Then her head broke the surface, eyes bulging in terror, trying desperately to cough out a lungful of poisoned water. The Minister's hands tightened on the wooden railing of his makeshift pulpit.

"She floats!" he bellowed. "Lord protect us, the woman is in league with Beelzebub!"

There was a roar of bloodlust from the crowd and one or two of the more theatrical ladies fell to the ground in a swoon, being careful not to land on the dirtiest patches.

Eufame McCalzean thrust her face heavenwards, gasping for air. With an agonized wail she began to tip backwards until her head was under the water again. A pocket of air trapped under her shift escaped in a large bubble and she sank below the surface once more. Her dainty feet, hands still tied to the ankles bobbed into view and floated for a few seconds before vanishing again.

"Is she guilty or not then?" one perplexed soldier grunted to the other, looking down at the ropes that would allow them to pull the woman to safety. They glanced uneasily at the Minister who stood rigid, eyes fixed on the loch, his face like thunder. Eufame's inability to simply sink or float was infuriating him. It was just like a woman to send out such mixed messages.

There was a sudden commotion from the front of the crowd. A dozen men had thrown off their hooded garbs and were rushing into the water. In the lead was Alexander Hepburn of Keith, lover of the unfortunate girl, followed by a handful of his rasher drinking companions.

The anguished young man reached the spot where Eufame had sank and dipped below the water, emerging with the gasping, choking woman in his arms. Her eyes were closed and black bile dribbled from her gaping mouth. He cut the bonds and, cradling her head in his hands, guided his half-conscious lover towards the shore. His companions had drawn cutlasses and pistols and now faced the Magistrate's soldiers.

Hepburn splashed onto the shore, hauling Eufame behind him, and his men formed a defensive circle around the soaking pair. They struggled up the bank, still dragging their burden and pushed their way through the crowd, which thronged tightly around them, hoping to get a closer look at the nearly drowned victim. The group had tethered their horses two hundred yards away to avoid suspicion and they headed in that direction, while the Magistrate's men dodged back and forth on the edge of the gathering, trying to get a clear shot.

The attempted rescue was as doomed as it was noble. Before Hepburn's group were half way to their steeds, a patrol was already galloping down from the castle to apprehend them.

In a few minutes it was all over. Alexander Hepburn and his men were surrounded and marched over to the Magistrate. Eufame was flung at the official's feet like a wet rag – blood and dirt blackening her once beautiful face. The Magistrate pursed his lips.

*"The woman lies before us," he said finally. "She did not sink."
He looked around at the uncomprehending soldiers.*

*"Therefore she is in league with the Devil!" The Minister finished
his colleague's sentence with an exasperated sigh.*

*"She did not sink because I rescued her!" Hepburn shouted.
"What is this madness?"*

*The Minister's head shot up and he looked malevolently at the
young man.*

*"As you are so quick to point out, Master Hepburn, you rescued
her," he spat. "Perhaps you too are an instrument of the Devil."*

*Alexander Hepburn was about to reply but his nearest companion
dug him violently in the ribs. The young man's eyes were bright with
fear. Like Eufame McCalzean he had not realised the gravity of this
situation. Looking down at the broken woman he was well aware of it
now.*

*Tears streamed down Alexander Hepburn's face, unnoticed among
the dirty streaks left by the Nor Loch. He tried to speak again but only
a choking sound came out. The Magistrate nodded to the soldiers who
roughly picked up the crying woman and marched her back towards
the castle.*

*Despite continued protestations of innocence, and the fact that she
was pregnant with her fourth child, Eufame McCalzean was strangled
outside the castle gates then burned at the stake.*

The term 'witch', which means to *twist or bend*, has its origins in
the ancient Anglo-Saxon word *Wicca* - originally derived from the
word *wise*. Witch is also related to the German word, *weihen* which
means *to consecrate or bless*.

Prior to the 14th century, witchcraft was regarded as a harmless
collection of beliefs and practices including healing through spells,
mixing ointments or concoctions, dabbling in the supernatural, divin-
ing or forecasting the future, and engaging in clairvoyance. Groups
holding to other beliefs, however, began to gradually brand witchcraft

as 'demon-worship.' – and with that definition the door that led to the torture chamber slowly creaked open.

The persecution of witchcraft lasted for centuries – a long and cruel mopping up of the last vestiges of Paganism. By medieval times most Pagans had either been absorbed into the Christian church or driven underground - and the majority of Western Europe converted to Catholicism. Not satisfied with that, the mainstream church now turned to weeding out anyone who didn't agree with their particular *brand* of religion and the sport of heretic burning was born. With this kind of religious fervour infecting the continent, anyone attached to old customs or markedly different in their thinking, was fair game to be turned into a human firework.

The Scots jumped on the persecution bandwagon late in the day but they certainly made up for lost time. The floodgates opened in the 16th century when Mary Queen of Scots arrived in Edinburgh from France to take over the Scottish throne. Along with other unsavoury foreign ideas, like escargot, she brought the 'Witchcraft Act' to Edinburgh. – which equated witchcraft with heresy and allowed the indiscriminate burning of either.

Her timing couldn't have been worse. Although Mary was a Catholic, southern Scotland, and especially Edinburgh, had been gripped by the spiritual zeal of Presbyterianism. The result was years of religious conflict between Presbyterians and Catholics - and open season on those who didn't seek the safety of either theological camp. Anyone you had a particular grudge against? If you couldn't legally pin a crime on them, you could always accuse them of casting a spell on your neighbour's cow.

And so the Scots wholeheartedly began the persecution of witches. Unlike the English they adopted torture as a means of interrogation – which certainly upped the number of confessions. They also burned their victims at the stake – a practice which was frowned on in the more civilized south.

The maltreatment of witches reached their zenith when Mary's son, James, was crowned. Brought up by Presbyterians, his religious enthusiasm already bordered on the obsessive when he travelled to Denmark to get married – and Denmark was a country which firmly believed in the evils of witchcraft.

Returning to Scotland with his bride, James encountered a violent storm near North Berwick, just off the coast of Edinburgh. Convinced that this was no ordinary tempest, but a plot by the Devil to sink himself and his bride, he instigated the infamous 'North Berwick Witch Trials'. Innocent men and women were tortured into confessing that they had conspired with 'Auld Nick' to cause the storm - including Eufame McCalzean, daughter of Lord Cliftonhall.

This incident turned James' morbid fascination with Satanic matters into a full blown fixation. Conveniently forgetting that traditional witchcraft had nothing to do with the Devil, he wrote a book called *Demonology* in 1597. This became required reading for future witch-hunters and incited a hysteria that lasted long after his death. In 1604 he became the first king of Britain and sparked off a wave of witch hunting in England as well.

The original Witchcraft Acts of Britain were not repealed until 1736 and less severe Witchcraft Acts lasted until 1951.

The Nor Loch's role in the detection of witches has become legendary but, in fact, there are few records of this kind of ordeal taking place. The normal method for gaining a conviction was to torture the witch (usually by sleep deprivation) until she admitted her guilt. These confessions could easily be backed up by the accusations of others (generated by malice or by torture) or the finding of Devil's Mark. And there weren't many in those unhygienic days that didn't have skin blemishes of some sort.

Happily, the number of witches killed in Scotland has probably been exaggerated. Although 20 000 is the usual figure bandied about, evidence has shown that about 4 000 people were accused of witchcraft and only 2/3 of those were executed – not that it's any consolation to those who were.

Edinburgh did stage a remarkable amount of witch hunts, however. Although there are no exact figures, it is estimated that around 300 witches and heretics were strangled then burned on Castlehill.

Today a small well at the end of the castle esplanade is the only monument to those unfortunate souls.

* * * *

There is a certain irony in the fact that traditional religions are now declining in Edinburgh. But Witchcraft, like Paganism, is enjoying a spectacular comeback, especially among younger people. In a way it's hardly surprising. Witches have a dozen modern Netflix series lauding their efforts as inspiration, while the Christian church has *Songs of Praise*.

Today witchcraft has been reinvented as *Wicca* – a neo-Pagan religion which practises a benevolent reverence for nature. The ever increasing amounts of people celebrating Edinburgh's Beltane Festival is testimony to Wicca's new high profile. The fact that large numbers of the revellers are not witches or Pagans shows that, to ordinary Scots, witchcraft is no longer something to be feared. In fact they are happy to tolerate any religion that actively encourages them to party.

Edinburgh, with its strong Pagan connections, has become something of a Wiccan Mecca. There are covens scattered about the city and even a Wiccan temple on display in the South Bridge, belonging to the 'Source Coven of the Blue Dragon'. In some of the little Old Town Streets you will find shops selling all things witchy – though you can usually buy a postcard of a Highland Coo there as well.

It has taken centuries for people to realise that being a witch isn't the same as being a Satanist - and that Pagans, far from being in league with the Devil, don't even believe in him. Wiccans don't criticize other religions, their spells and rituals are designed to increase harmony with the world and Wiccan Law has a rather simple tenant which centuries of Christianity would have done well to heed.

And ye harm none.

So witchcraft is flourishing in Edinburgh but there doesn't seem to be anything particularly supernatural or frightening about that. Then again, there never really was – it's just an ages old prejudice. Edinburgh's reputation may seem a little more sinister because of its associations with modern Wiccans but that's an unfair connection.

On the other hand, all religions can become perverted. The idea of Christianity, after all, is to love your neighbour. Not to love your neighbour if he's like you, otherwise kill him.

Practised as they are meant to be, both Witchcraft and Christianity are benevolent ideologies, designed to help rather than harm. But both have an opposite side, still little understood and feared to this day.

Christianity has Satanism

Witchcraft has Black Magic

Chapter 5

Magic

One man's "magic" is another man's engineering.

Robert A Heinlein

In 1987 a student called Paul Whitton was working as a domestic at Edinburgh Royal Infirmary, when he met a teenage co-worker called Rose. They were often on the same shifts and, naturally, ended up talking. After a few fascinating conversations about which solvents removed the toughest stains and the most unusual places they had ever found effluence, he asked her out for a drink. Rose accepted.

There were things regarding his work companion Paul wasn't crazy about. She claimed to have psychic powers for one thing, which he considered as believable an assertion as being abducted by aliens. Apart from that they got on well, and one date led to another and then another.

Paul liked to think he was a man of the world and, after several pints of Tenants, he boldly asked the young lady if she wanted to go back to his place. After all, he had a mini-bar.

Rose looked at him sadly and explained that she couldn't. She had an ex-boyfriend who was extremely jealous of their relationship.

33

Recovering from the shock that he might actually be in a relation-ship, Paul pointed out that 'ex' meant just that. What exactly did this former boyfriend intend to do?

"He's already done it," Rose said. "He put a curse on you."

Paul quickly ordered a vodka.

Rose explained that her boyfriend was a magician. A black magi-cian. The curse was a roundabout one, a way of showing his power. He told Rose he had raised a demon to do his bidding and installed it in Paul's house. It would ensure that she would never be allowed to stay with the would-be lothario. In fact, no female would.

Paul had heard plenty of excuses why girls couldn't come home with him but this took the biscuit. Rose excused herself and left. A few days later she handed in her notice at work and Paul never saw her again.

He paid little attention to the supposed curse on his house – he had enough trouble just paying the rent without worrying about unwanted lodgers. Besides, he was only in the flat for the summer. It didn't take him long to meet someone else – Jane - and she seemed perfectly hap-py to stay there.

At first.

Paul Whitton had a room in a large, Victorian two story flat in Spottiswood Street, Marchmont. The house was normally occupied by a group of students but they had gone for the summer holidays and he was looking after the place in exchange for cheap rent. Since he was alone in this huge house for three months, he offered to let his new girlfriend use the flat whenever she liked.

At first, she did.

Then Jane began meeting him from work rather than waiting for him at home. She wanted to go out at every opportunity. She tried eve-ry trick to get him to stay at her own small, rather untidy flat. One day he arrived back home to find her pacing up and down in the kitchen trembling. A nearby ashtray overflowed with cigarette butts.

"Look, I know I haven't washed any dishes for a week," he said. "And some of them may have gone a bit mouldy…"

Jane ignored his protests and dragged him upstairs. He would have thought this quite promising if his bedroom hadn't been on the bottom level.

"Watch," she said.

She opened one of the bedroom doors and pulled him back down the stairs. As soon as they reached the bottom, they heard the upstairs door slam shut.

"It's just the wind," said Paul.

"You think Hurricane Betty's outside or something? All the windows are closed!" Jane marched up the stairs and opened the bedroom door again. She came half way back down then stopped. "It won't slam until I reach the telephone table at the bottom of the stairs," she announced confidently.

She started down again. As she stepped off the bottom step the door slammed.

"Watch the telephone."

The telephone rang. Paul Whitton almost jumped out of his skin. He grabbed the phone and held it to his ear. Jane lit another cigarette.

"Someone's laughing on the line, aren't they?"

"It might just be… interference."

But it didn't sound like interference. Paul Whitton replaced the receiver and looked up the stairs. The landing seemed much darker than usual, as if something bulky was squatting, just out of sight, blocking the light.

"Honey I think you're great," Jane said. "Much nicer than my last boyfriend. But he only needed a cleaner. You need an exorcist. So long."

And she left.

Paul Whitton tried the experiment with the bedroom door many times. If he left it closed, he would hear it open when he reached the bottom of the stairs. If he opened it, he would hear it slam. The phone would ring in the middle of the night and eventually he didn't dare answer it because he knew what he would hear. If any of his male friends called, he could talk to them without a problem. If there was a female voice on the other end the phone would immediately go dead – even telephone saleswomen couldn't get through.

But, worst of all, was the dark at the top of the stairs. No matter how bright a light bulb burned up there or how much sunlight filled the big Victorian flat, it always looked as if something was lurking on the landing, just around the corner. And Paul always felt there was it was looking down on him, whenever he used the phone. He would have shifted the telephone somewhere else but there was only one socket in the house.

When he moved to his new place in September, he kicked over the telephone table, gave the landing an offensive sign and ran out of the front door.

Nicky Harrington was the first of the regular tenants to come back from her holidays, moving in the day after Paul left. That night she was sitting in the kitchen drinking a mug of tea when the telephone rang. She went to the bottom of the stairs and answered it. There was nothing but an ominous crackling on the line. It sounded a little like laughter.

As she sat there a horrible feeling crept over her – a certainty that something was watching her from the top landing. With a shudder she retreated to the kitchen and made herself another brew.

Suddenly there was a crash from above and a thundering noise erupted over her head. Nicky looked up at the ceiling

It was shaking. There was something so heavy running across the floor of the upstairs bedroom that she could actually see the vibra-tions. The bouncing kitchen light went out with a pop and the room was plunged into darkness. Nicky leapt to her feet. She wasn't the type to panic - there was an intruder in the house so it was essential she get out.

She fumbled her way from the kitchen, hit the hall light and headed for the front door. As she passed the telephone table, the bedroom door upstairs flew open with a bang. Nicky screamed. The telephone rang. She leapt away from it. The doorbell rang. Wide eyed with terror, she yanked the front door open.

It was Paul Whitton.

"I left some stuff here, so I came to collect it." he said. "You look a bit peaky."

Nicky hauled Paul up the stairs. He was getting used to this by now.

They searched all the upstairs rooms. There was nobody else in the house. But in one bedroom a wardrobe lay on its side, one of the doors hanging off.

"You been spring cleaning?" Paul asked.

"Your stuff's in that wardrobe," Nicky said. "And it was upright a couple of minutes ago."

Paul Whitton took his things and never came back.

This account of the 'Marchmont Chaperone' has never been published before. It's one of many similar stories I've heard living in Edinburgh - most told to me long before I started writing or had anything to do with the supernatural.

This particular incident was recounted to me by the people involved – people I once knew well. Except for Rose, of course, who nobody ever saw again. One became a social worker, one a businessman and one a scientist. Two came to believe that the whole thing had been a product of student life – in other words, too much alcohol and over active imaginations. The third is convinced that Rose's ex-boyfriend really was a magician who put a curse on the house.

Guess which one?

The scientist.

In the 21st century it is easy to scoff at the methods once employed for seeking out dabblers in the black arts. But are we any further forwards? Would you know a black witch if you saw one?

Actually, you probably would. Modern Wiccans aren't shy about telling you of their religious persuasion - I can honestly see the day when we'll have Jehovah's Wiccans knocking on doors.

But what exactly is magic? And why are we afraid of it?

When I refer to magic, I'm talking about a whole host of practices – including White, Green, Grey and Folk Magic. The one thing they have in common is that they are all 'good' in their outlook. Black Magic, however, is a perversion of magic rather than a type. In the same way, you can lump Benedictines, Franciscans, Episcopalians and Presbyterians under the term 'Christian' – but you don't include Satanists.

So we'll get to the Black Arts later.

Let's deal with 'good' magic first.

'Magik' has been with us from the beginnings of mankind. The ancient cave paintings in France may not just portray successful hunts – it is likely they were used in conjunction with dances and chants to actually try and produce kills.

As the nomadic life of early humans became an agricultural one, both the civic and spiritual lives of these simple people evolved to fit their new society. Tribal elders, controlling a more and more complex civilization, increased in numbers and became bureaucrats. And tribal shamans, who communicated with the spirit world, evolved into priests.

It was at this point that magic and religion began to diverge. Originally the shaman's task was to negotiate between his tribe and the spirit world – and he did this on behalf of the community. They asked for things like plentiful food or a mild winter and the Shaman had a word with the sprits to see if they could arrange it.

As 'proper' religions began to form, this procedure was reversed. Now the gods wanted things and the priests' role was to let his flock know exactly how they could please the deities.

This new method of spiritual communication was a lot less people friendly, but it certainly didn't do the priests any harm. While they were asking the populace for things to appease their God, they could stick in a few suggestions from their own personal wish list. Like a nice new chariot or a couple of slaves. Personal acts of magic were replaced by highly elaborate rituals, such as the funeral rites of the Egyptians and the sacrifice rituals of the Babylonians, Persians, Aztecs and Mayans

Simple magic allowed individuals with no power or social standing a direct access to the gods and it wasn't surprising then more powerful men in society became unhappy with this communion between deity and common plebe. As priesthoods became increasingly powerful, magic became more and more frowned upon.

The stage was set for the eradication of magical belief and practice all over the world – from the appropriation of Pagan holidays by the Catholic Church to the burning of witches outside Edinburgh Castle.

It's an attitude that persists to this day, and not only in the Christian world. Muslims, for instance, believe in magic but forbid its practice.

The fact remains that organized religion and magic have the same origins. Religion might have become dominant it couldn't entirely vanquish its more primitive sibling. In fact they remained much closer than many might believe. Fasting, prayers, the Sacrament, exorcisms and using the holy names of God to repel demons, all have a whiff of old style magic about them - and none are far removed from primitive incantations and rituals. Medieval authors, under the control of the Church, compiled wonderlores and collections of spells. During the early Middle Ages miraculous tales were told of the power of saintly relics to work miracles.

St Giles' 14th century Cathedral, right in the heart of Edinburgh, is a perfect example of this. It once possessed an arm bone belonging to St Giles himself, a relic said to have miraculous healing properties. A magic bone. And take a look at the roof if you go in there. You'll see dozens of 'Green Men' carved into the arches – Pagan symbols of fertility that were still part of church iconography when the cathedral was built.

Magic's great enemy wasn't the church – religion might want to destroy wizards and witches but at least it took them seriously. However, after thousands of years of uneasy co-existence, both magic and religion came up against a new enemy. Religion tackled this threat with its usual dogmatic belligerence but, this time, the adversary had an equally powerful weapon. Logic.

It was called science.

To a certain extent the motivation behind religion, magic and science is the same – they are all methods of discerning the underlying reality behind what we can see with our own eyes. For millennium all the accepted explanations came from religion - and woe betide anyone who disagreed. Many fledgling scientists suffered the same fate as Pagans, heretics and witches - look at the punishments meted out to the first men to suggest earth revolved round the sun.

But science was offering a fundamentally different interpretation of reality from the spiritual one offered by religion or magic. A fascinating interpretation. An infectious interpretation. And perhaps, significantly, it wasn't forcing anyone to accept its conclusions. In the end, the scientists won hands down, as public opinion slowly but inexorably shifted their way.

The ever changing scientific carrot, no matter how unpalatable, had beaten the inflexible theological stick.

For a while magic fared no better than religion in this conflict. Like science, magic holds that an undiscovered reality may have laws and principles which it is possible to discover and control. But science, once it blossomed, began to show more and more spectacular results. Its adherents had the ability to continually revise and correct mistakes - which is a good job, since no witch ever made a plague virus. The result, inevitably, was that scientific method replaced its more mystic counterparts. Astrology turned into astronomy and alchemy into chemistry.

Over the centuries, magic did enjoy small resurgences. In the late 19th century. Spiritualism came into being and for a short while enjoyed massive popularity. Edinburgh had its own Spiritualist champion in the writer Sir Arthur Conan Doyle – who was instrumental in boosting its popularity in Britain.

Colonialism put westerners in contact with India and Egypt and re-introduced exotic beliefs to Europe. This gave rise to magical organizations like the Theosophical Society and the Hermetic Order of the Golden Dawn, which attracted celebrities like William Butler Yeats, Algernon Blackwood and Arthur Machen.

Magic enjoyed a British revival in the 1950's, with the repeal of the last Witchcraft Act in 1951. Gerald Gardner, now recognised as the founder of Wicca, began to publish *Witchcraft Today* soon after. The sexual revolution of the sixties, drug culture and even feminism fuelled this new religion and its variations.

* * * *

In the 21st century, magic is now more popular than ever and magicians and witches feature heavily as the heroes of TV and film. The Bible may be the world's best-selling book but the planet's most popular fictional character is a wizard by the name of Harry Potter – created, of course, in Edinburgh.

The Christian church finally bowed to the idea of natural selection and realised its only chance of survival was to evolve. Women and gay men are slowly working their way towards being treated as equals. Better late than never, I suppose. Attitudes towards sex are being relaxed. The church accepts that many want to worship God in their own way – not as some Gandalf look-alike, but a divinity in a form and shape of their own choosing.

Only it's too late. There is a religion and a practice which has always encouraged these things. Paganism and magic.

On the other hand, science seems to have developed into a discipline based on faith. Personally I don't see the difference between going to confession and going to a psychotherapist – except a priest doesn't charge you £20 an hour. Only a handful of people really understand what black holes, memes or quarks are and quantum physics is as mysterious as the Holy Grail. Yet millions accept that scientific theories are the keys to understanding existence – even though we don't have a clue how they work.

In a way, this is the ultimate irony. The rules of science have become so vague, flexible and, on occasion, downright unbelievable, that science and magic have begun to blend.

An example? Scientists have recently suggested that all matter is made of particles so small that they don't really exist. If that isn't a magical explanation for the universe, I don't know what is.

What's more, science has not produced the rewards it once promised. On the contrary, it's thanks to scientists that we've replaced bows and arrows with nuclear warheads. We live in a world threatened by global pollution. And millions are still starving.

Religion has lost its hold and science has lost its shine. So what's left?

White magic now finds itself in an astonishing position – whether its practices really work or not, people are willing to give them a try. There is a cultural and sociological flexibility to magic that organized religion doesn't condone and an inherent respect for nature that science has never shown.

Magic is slowly becoming respectable again.

* * * *

So far, I have only written about 'good' magic, but that's because most practitioners follow this 'right' path. It can be split into several categories.

"Green magic" involves the practitioner's attuning himself or herself to nature. "White magic" is where the practitioner concentrates on the needs of human society and attempts to meet them. "Grey magic" replaces the absolute stand of these established colours with an ethical code that is particular to the practitioner. "Folk magic" is an eclectic collection of herbalism, faith healing, curses and hexes, candle magic and other workings, that thrived in rural areas for centuries.

The basic mechanism of magical practices is the spell, a spoken or written formula used in conjunction with a particular set of ingredients. In a way it is similar to uttering a prayer and using religious props like a prayer shawl, mat or rosary. The difference is that prayers are not guaranteed to work. To the magician, however, if a spell is cast properly, it will succeed. If it doesn't, either the spell is a fake or it has not been executed properly.

I don't know how many covens there are in Edinburgh - they don't exactly put adverts in the local paper looking for members. Actually, sometimes they do. But there are a considerable number and that figure is growing all the time. Practitioners now come from all walks of life and occupations – I even met a lawyer who is a witch. I was warier of the fact that he was a lawyer.

So Edinburgh has a magical side too. But is it a black magical side?

The broad definition of 'Black' Magic is that it draws power from or invokes demons, devils, or spirits of chaos and destruction. It can be used with the intent of injuring or killing someone for the personal gain of the practitioner.

All white magic tries to be in tune with nature but black magicians want power over nature, not harmony with it. The earliest black magicians had no scientific concept of how nature worked – so it was a fair assumption that the way to force nature to one's will was to do the opposite of what white witches were doing.

The most obvious way to achieve this was to take traditional Pagan rituals and reverse them. This is also a tactic used by Satanists, with their black candles, inverted crosses and backwards mass.

I talked to several Wiccans and asked if there was any black magic going on in the city. They assured me that there was, but black magicians practised alone and in secrecy. No one would give me any names and one or two suggested that I really shouldn't pry any further.

I did, but I still couldn't find anyone who'd admit to being a Black Magician. Then again, I'm no Woodward and Bernstein. They're probably out there.

But how dangerous are they? Is there any real menace from black magic?

It doesn't really seem so. Like the religions it inspired, magic appears to function best as a belief system. You can pray to God for a Porsche or you can make a few incantations in front of your local car dealership but neither is likely to get you the vehicle of your dreams.

In places like Haiti and Africa there is a body of evidence that indicates curses and black magic spells actually harm people. But acceptance of magic as an actual force is much stronger there. If your victim truly believes in a death curse it may just be enough to kill him – the opposite of faith healing in a way. Like organized religion, it is a matter of conviction.

It seems this conviction is beyond our 'civilized' city. There may be a lot of scantily clad people in Edinburgh running round singing to the trees but the city hasn't suddenly turned into a Shangri-La. There may be some warlocks in dark cellars trying to put the evil eye on overbearing authority but there aren't any councillors dropping dead in the streets. Which is a shame.

Edinburgh, quite rightly, has a magical connection and that has added to its sinister reputation. But magic looks to be more bark than bite.

Of course I could be barking up the wrong tree myself. Perhaps we should look at the definition again of black magic again and its correlation to modern science.

It draws power from or invokes spirits of chaos and destruction. It can be used with the intent of injuring or killing someone or for the personal gain of the practitioner.

Nuclear weapons, anyone?

Chapter 6

Satanism

I do not fear Satan *half so much as I fear those who fear him.*

St. Teresa of Avila

The young gentlewoman glanced nervously behind her. She had not come far and didn't have far to go, but the hour was late. She had been attending to her husband's niece who was in labour in a small apartment in Castlehill. The niece had been nervous, cold to touch, her skin clammy. Though she had a midwife, the poor girl had cried considerably, for it was her first child and all women knew the dangers of childbirth. Mortality rates were high - for new mothers as well as their offspring.

Because of this the gentlewoman was out much later than she would have liked and silently thanked the saints that she had a maid with her. She would have preferred her husband or one of his footmen to be her guardian – someone with a sword and dagger – but they were drawing close to home.

The gentlewoman turned into the Bowhead and looked down the steep winding street to her home in the Grassmarket. The West Bow was impossibly steep – horses could not pull carts up it and even riders struggled to urge their mounts up the muddy incline from bottom to top. Usually they had to dismount.

47

At this hour, however, there were no horses. On either side, tenements rose from the narrow street, almost blocking out the night sky. Between their lofty forms a pale moon hovered over rickety Grassmarket lands, obscured by the palls of smoke from the dark houses in the foreground. There were a few drunken forms slouched in the shadows of doorways and one or two sprawled on the ground. Further down the hill two inebriated Newhaven fishwives slipped and slid in the mud, laughing deliriously, still dragging their creels behind them.

A window creaked open far above. The gentlewoman looked up but saw nothing but night.

"Gardee Loo!" a sleepy voice shouted and the gentlewoman flattened herself against the wall. There was a hiss and a wet slopping sound as a bucketful of sewage landed at her feet. The maid skipped away, skidded in the mud and landed flat on her back. The gentlewoman tisked.

Half way down the hill, lights suddenly went on across the street, cutting a yellow swathe through the darkness. The gentlewoman looked up, surprised.

The lights in the house were constant and bright, not the normal splutter of candles lit by tapers or lamps filled with animal fat. She could see a group of women in the lit windows laughing and clapping their hands. The gentlewomen tutted again for the women were not dressed properly – she caught a glimpse of bare shoulder.

The door below the windows opened and more light spilled out, but only for a second, for a huge figure unfolded into the darkness - blocking out the illumination. The gentlewoman's eyes widened and her maid gave a gasp of horror.

The stranger was at least ten feet tall.

The maid gathered up her skirts and prepared to run, but the gentlewoman placed a stern hand on her arm. She was a lady and ladies did not run. God was on her side. She turned and continued walking down the street, trying not to fall, dragging the maid forcefully along. The giant, who they could now see was female, kept pace with them, taking one slow stride for each three of theirs, glaring balefully across the narrow street. Despite her pride the gentlewoman quickened her pace. The maid, stumbling along next to her was making small sobbing noises and staring pointedly at the ground.

Suddenly the giantess swerved and vanished into the dark hole of one of the many narrow closes that lined the West Bow. The maid gave a loud sigh and crossed herself.

The gentlewoman slapped her hand. "Less of your Papish gestures," she snapped. Her dander up, she left the terrified girl and strode across the road to the entrance of the close.

Suddenly she drew back with a gasp, hand over her mouth.

It wasn't the smell, but what she had seen.

The close was filled with flaming torches, as if a great crowd had gathered there. Yet the woman couldn't see any people. She narrowed her eyes trying to discern shapes, but there were none. Then the noise came – a high roll of laughter rippling through the alley – sick and gurgling and high pitched.

It wasn't the sound of human laughter.

The gentlewoman's courage ebbed away. She turned and hurried back to the crying maid and they made their way silently home.

That night she lay in bed, wide awake. The monster roamed through her thoughts and the invisible laughter rang unhealthily in her head. But something else nagged at her. Something she found even harder to accept than the apparitions she had seen.

The next day she retraced her steps, still accompanied by the reluctant maid. When they got to the entrance of the close, she nodded solemnly.

She had been right. The troll woman and the invisible torch bearers had all been gathered around the entrance of one specific dwelling.

It belonged to Major Thomas Weir, the respected Presbyterian preacher.

Major Thomas Weir is Edinburgh's most famous witch, as well as the city's best known Satanist. Closer inspection of the known facts, however, prove he was neither. But whatever his true conduct in life, Thomas Weir certainly turned into one of Edinburgh's most legendary ghosts.

Part of his notoriety, no doubt, comes from the fact that he was one of the few *men* in Edinburgh to be executed as a witch. And the shock value is doubled when you consider that he was also a respected minister.

Thomas Weir was born around 1600, rose to the rank of Major in the Earl of Lanark's regiment and commanded Edinburgh's City Guard. A strict Presbyterian, he fought with the Covenanters when they rebelled against Charles I. It was he who famously led Presbyterian turned Royalist, the Marquis of Montrose, to his death by beheading outside St Giles' Cathedral. While the Marquis accepted his fate with dignity and grace, Weir taunted him with shouts of 'Dog, Atheist, and Traitor'.

Bit of a dick then.

There were also rumours that Weir used his religious standing to visit married women in their chambers, when their husbands weren't at home. But the Presbyterians had long been the most powerful force in Scotland and such was Weir's reputation that nobody dared level any serious accusations against him.

Weir lived with his sister, Jean, in Anderson's Close in the West Bow, the area which is now Victoria Street. This was the neighbourhood favoured by a group of zealous Presbyterians known as the Bowhead Saints and Weir's religious fanaticism earned him the pious nickname 'Evangelical Thomas'.

Then came the incident with the flaming torches and the giant woman outside his house.

What really went on that night will never be known. The story was made popular by Professor George Sinclair in his 1685 bestseller *Satan's Invisible World Discovered*. But it was written fifteen years after the incident was supposed to take place and Sinclair's lurid bestseller is a dubious source, as we shall discover later.

Whatever transpired that night, even if it was just a malicious rumour spread by those who disliked Weir, it certainly had a startling effect.

A short time afterwards, at one of his regular prayer meetings Weir stood up and began to confess to a whole plethora of unsavoury activities. He admitted to numerous affairs, bestiality and a host of lesser crimes. He also claimed to have been sleeping with his sister for forty years. These revelations, especially his bad taste in sexual partners, rocked the Presbyterian community. Weir was arrested along with his poor sister.

If Weir's confessions had shocked Edinburgh, his sister's tale really sealed his fate. She claimed that the carved walking stick he carried everywhere had been given to him by the Devil and had black magic powers. Other condemnations soon came thick and fast, from witnesses who claimed to have been too afraid to speak out the time. Anything odd about his character was now paraded forth as proof of his Devil worship.

The testimony of his sister was by far the most damming and included revelations that they had ridden in a carriage that only the two of them could see. Far-fetched as this invisible taxi might seem, Weir was burned alive at Gallowlea, now the top of Leith Walk. Jean didn't last much longer and was executed soon after.

Almost immediately the ghost stories began. Lights were regularly seen burning inside Weir's empty house and loud laughter could be heard in the dwelling – giving the premises an instant haunted reputation. The idea of squatters capitalising on an empty dwelling in overcrowded Edinburgh was obviously never considered.

Others claimed to have seen 'the Wizard of the West Bow', as he was now called, riding out of Anderson's Close at night on a headless horse and then turning down the West Bow into the Grassmarket. Presumably it had memorised the route.

These Sleepy Hollowesque activities caused his home to be known as the 'Haunted Close' from that point. Occasionally, the dead major was witnessed riding a coach drawn by six black horses – perhaps it was a special occasion.

The house was not officially occupied again until the 18th century, when a former soldier named William Patullo moved in. His military training hadn't prepared Mr Patullo for finding a 'ghostly calf' (yes, really) at the bottom of his bed and he quickly moved out again.

The house reputedly stayed empty from then on (though it was used in a commercial capacity) until the building was demolished in 1827.

Was Weir a real witch and in league with the Devil? No. In fact he wasn't even convicted of witchcraft or devil worship but bestiality and incest, which is bad enough, I suppose. His sister was the one accused of dabbling in the black arts – though she was torched because of the incest charge as well.

It is likely that Weir was no more than a guilt ridden and demented old man. His sister had been the bed partner of her own brother and her mental state was very much in question too.

But it was the politics of the day that really damned Weir. By the time he confessed to his crimes the Presbyterian movement, of which he was a leading light, was suffering immense persecution at the orders of Charles II. That very year, all Presbyterian ministers had been ordered to leave the city.

Weir was in his seventies by this point and must have known he had little time left. His beloved religion was destroyed and he was being forced to abandon his home. His confession may have been the last chance at rebellion from a beaten old man.

All the legends of witchcraft and Satanism attached to his name could just be anti-Presbyterian propaganda. But they stuck.

Major Weir is the most famous example but, from the mid-15th century to the 18th century, inquisitors seemed to find Devil worshipers everywhere – a task which was greatly aided by the fact that they could torture their suspects into confessing, or damn them without any proper evidence of wrongdoing.

The percentage of those accused who actually attempted to worship the Devil is probably tiny and Satanism, as an organized activity, was almost non-existent before the 17th century.

Edinburgh's notorious 18th century sex and drinking clubs put on pseudo ritualistic orgies, with overtones of Devil worship - but they were flirting with Satan rather than getting into bed with him. These societies were really excuses for rich immature men to indulge in drinking, outrageous behaviour and sexual role playing. If that's a real Satanist club then so was Stringfellows.

There were a few genuinely Satanic organisations in the 19th century, such as the Society for the Reparation of Souls and the Church of Carmel – and both were in France. These groups reportedly performed black masses - the prayer was recited backwards, the crucifix was upside down, the Eucharist was defiled and the rite ended in a sexual orgy. They are also said to have practised human sacrifice.

The 20th century saw the rise to fame of Aleister Crowley, who lived at Loch Ness. He called himself 'the beast' and was very complimentary about the Lord of Darkness, but still peeved about being labelled a Satanist. He and his followers were far more interested in black magic and the occult.

The largest Satanic movement began in the 1960's in the United States – the *Church of Satan*, founded by Anton Szandor LaVey. La Vey was hardly the typical portrait of a Devil worshipper – among his other jobs he was lion tamer, a piano accompanist to Marilyn Monroe and a crime photographer with the San Francisco police department. He quit because he was disgusted with the violence that he had seen, but it had affected him more deeply than he realised. He began to think that man's true nature was a mixture of lust, pride, hedonism and wilfulness, and that these attributes enabled the advancement of civilization. From there it was a short step to concluding that flesh should not be denied but celebrated, and individuals who stand in the way of achieving what one wants should be severely dissuaded. To his credit, however, he never conducted a black mass and deplored the use of black magic for criminal activity.

Well, everyone has a nice side.

La Vey loved ritual, ceremony and pageantry – and media coverage. He even allegedly portrayed Satan in the film 'Rosemary's Baby'. He died in 1997, but the church of Satan is still going strong – along with other offshoots like the Temple of Set.

These large organised Satanic cults have never shied away from the media. If their members indulged in human sacrifice or the physical destruction of their enemies, they would not have lasted – but as far as anyone can see they aren't breaking any laws. Activities like Black Masses or orgies may be highly distasteful to the more responsible members of society but freedom of expression is supposed to be what good guys embrace.

The philosophy of mainstream Satanist groups is suspect, but hardy terrifying. Many see the Devil merely as a symbol of the liberation of mankind - the champion of individuality if you like. The Temple of Set emphasizes 'rational self-interest' and taking responsibility for one's own intellectual and ethical decisions. The Church of Satan even sets out rules for its members - which, admittedly, isn't a very individualistic thing to do.

1 Do not give opinions or advice unless you are asked.

2 Do not tell your troubles to others unless you are sure that they want to hear them.

3 When in another's lair, show him respect or else do not go there.

4 If a guest in your lair annoys you, treat him cruelly and without mercy.

5 Do not make sexual advances unless you are given the mating signal.

6 Do not take that which does not belong to you unless it is a burden to the person and he cries out to be relieved.

7 Acknowledge the power of magic if you have used it successfully to obtain your desires. If you deny the power of magic after having called upon it with success, you will lose all you have obtained.

8 Do not complain about anything to which you need not subject yourself.

9 Do not harm little children.

10 Do not kill non-human animals unless attacked or for your food.

11 When walking in open territory, bother no one. If someone bothers you, ask him to stop. If he does not stop, destroy him.

Not exactly a shopping list for evil is it? Rules number 4 and 11 are a bit harsh, but not compared to the Bible's 2nd commandment, which advocates punishing children for the sins of their grandfathers.

The real danger comes from smaller groups of Satanists – those whose members seem to have a high proportion of disturbed teenagers, psychopaths and heavy metal aficionados. These cults really do worship the Devil as an entity and rumours abound of their members practising animal mutilation and ritual murder. Oddly enough these groups are despised by mainstream Satanists – who seem to be unaware of the incongruity in that attitude.

The sad fact is, those who want to indulge in such sordid practices will do so no matter what. If they didn't believe in Satan, they'd be killing people because they couldn't get a library card. All in all, it hasn't got much to do with the Prince of Darkness, if he exists at all.

Edinburgh has often been portrayed as a place where dubious groups wear black robes and chant round pentangles in dark basements. I've never found any Devil worshiping sects in Edinburgh – there isn't even an Edinburgh University Satanic Society and they'll start any kind of club that allows them to drink. I only tracked down one genuine Satanist, who claimed to be a member of a cult called the 'Brimstone Shrine'. I was scared, I'll admit - but that was because I thought he might stab me at any moment - not because he was pals with the Devil.

Like Black Magicians, Edinburgh's reputation for Satanic goings on appears to stem from mixing up Devil worshippers with Wiccans and Pagans. Auld Hairy himself doesn't seem to be around.

Then again, I keep remembering the line from the movie *The Usual Suspects*.

The greatest trick the Devil ever played was convincing the world that he didn't exist.

Perhaps the same applies to truly Satanic or occult groups. If they really were up to something odd, the last thing they would do is advertise the fact – or even the reality of their existence.

And Edinburgh *is* the sort of city to have such cults. It's old, it's secretive and it has a long, whispered history of clandestine societies.

So who are they?

Chapter 7

Dark Secrets

The secret of my influence has always been fact that it remained secret.

Salvador Dali

The midge filled air reeked with the stench of sweat, fear and death. Men hacked at each other with axes and broadswords and chunks of flesh, bone glistening through the bloody meat, flew from mutilated bodies. Knights struggled in agony as their dying mounts crushed the armour onto their broken torsos. Whinnying horses and screaming soldiers were drowned out by the roars of bloodlust and the crash of metal upon metal.

That morning the English army had begun crossing the gorge at Bannock Burn and lining up opposite a ragged but determined Scots army. The Scots had 13,000 men. Edward II of England was leading an army of 40,000. He had expected his enemy to run when they saw the forest of English banners, but the Scots were fighting for their independence. They weren't going anywhere.

There was a disturbance at the head of Edward's army - the cavalry had become incensed at the impertinence of such a small, badly equipped force. Instead of waiting for the foot soldiers to cross the gorge, they drew their swords and charged.

Massive warhorses laden with armour rumbled across the flat marshy field towards the Scots, their thundering hooves sending up fountains of dirty water. The Scots grimly raised their fifteen foot pikes as the accelerating tide of muscle and metal swept towards them.

An unstoppable force met an immovable object. Scots soldiers were flung backwards into the air, their limbs snapping like twigs, as the first line of horses impaled themselves on the pikes. English knights flew over the manes of their steeds and into the enemy ranks, where they were hacked to pieces.

Now the second line of cavalry was trying to urge their mounts forward but dozens of horses were impaled on the human barrier, writhing and screeching among the bristling mass of Scots pikes. Petrified chargers fought to retreat from the carnage in front of them, rearing up and throwing their riders, or turning and colliding with other animals.

Unable to get near the Scots line, the back ranks of knights milled around in confusion. From the other side of the gorge the English archers unleashed a curtain of arrows at an enemy, but the Scots were obscured by the mass of cavalry. The archers misjudged the distance and a many of the English knights fell from their mounts, cut down in a deadly shower unleashed by their own side.

The cavalry backed away and tried to regroup but, to Edward's horror, the Scots picked up their pikes and began to advance. In perfect formation they marched steadily towards the Bannock Burn gorge, driving the English in front of them.

The cavalry charged again and again, but they had been thrown into disarray. There was no longer enough space to gather the momentum required to smash the Scottish line. In alarm they turned and galloped back to the Bannock Burn.

The bulk of the English army had descended into the ravine and were struggling up the other side when they found themselves confronted by their own retreating cavalry. Foot soldiers were swept aside by the bloody flanks of the massive chargers or trampled underfoot, until their sheer numbers clogged the horses' flight.

The gorge was a struggling throng of trapped and frantic bodies when the Scots reached it. They plunged their pikes into the front line of the enemy, drew their weapons and charged.

Within minutes the ravine was filled with dead and dying men - and the burn ran scarlet as both sides hacked and tore at each other.

The English had been completely outmanoeuvred but they vastly outnumbered the Scots. They were better equipped, better armed and better trained and, slowly, these advantages began to tell. Knights in full armour swung with great broadswords, slicing through the Scots' leather tunics and parting arms and heads from bodies. The English foot soldiers began to find their rhythm, countering the Scots wild slicing with short strokes and quick parries.

Eventually they forced the northern army back over the lip of the gorge.

Walter de Baston galloped out of the gory chasm, Edward's banner raised over his head. He was followed by a tide of howling men who had fought their way up the right flank of the Scottish force and gained the top of the slope.

Baston looked at the flat land to his right, free of enemy forces. If he could rally his men here, they had space to win back some semblance of formation. Shouting and waving the banner, gesticulating frantically, he began to coax his soldiers into lines.

It was working! As they fought, his men were instinctively shuffling into rows, defending their neighbours as well as themselves. Soon he would be able to outflank the enemy and turn this carnage back into a proper battle. He would lead his men in a scything action round the back of the Scots force and trap them between two fronts.

Grinning, De Baston wiped the grime from his eyes and looked towards the woods at the base of Coxet Hill - gauging how long his arc would have to be to contain the entire Scots army.

The smile froze on his face.

"Holy mother of God."

A line of mounted men had appeared on the crest of the hill. They wore full armour, not leather and iron studs like the other Scots nobles, but shining breastplates over chain mail. Their horses were draped with white mantles and, above their heads, banners and pennants fluttered – each emblazoned with the same mark. De Baston recognised it at once. The Cross Pattee. The eight pointed cross.

The symbol of the Knights Templar.

The mounted men drew their gleaming swords and began to move down the hill. De Bastion looked at his exhausted soldiers struggling to hold their line. He knew the legends of these 'Knights of God' – had heard them since he was a child. They were the Holy knights. The Christian Knights.

The Invincible Knights

He crossed himself, tugged his mount round and galloped back into the chasm. His men watched in astonishment until they too saw the force descending the hill.

They broke ranks and fled.

Within minutes the entire English army was struggling to escape up the other side of the Bannock Burn ravine, trampling each other into the mud, drowning in the river under the weight of their own armour. The Scots roared in triumph and gave chase, gleefully hacking chunks out of the enemy's backs as they ran.

The Templars reached the bottom of the hill, emerged from the trees and slowed to a halt. A hulking Scots noble, his beard matted

*with blood, galloped over on a small sweating charger. His scarred
face was jubilant*

*"You have helped us win our freedom this day," he shouted. "You
have the everlasting thanks of Robert De Brus and I pledge you protection throughout my kingdom." He grinned maniacally and repeated
the phrase.*

"My Kingdom."

*The Templars raised their swords in salute, wheeled their mounts
round and rode back into the trees.*

There is an old legend about Bannockburn, the battle that won
Scotland its independence. The Scots and English armies had been
fighting for hours and though the English had suffered heavy casual-
ties, they were by no means beaten.

According to lore, the Auld Enemy were horrified to see another
Scottish force suddenly appear on a nearby hill. This definitely wasn't
cricket. They turned and ran, without realizing this second 'army'
were only local villagers waiting to scavenge among the dead bodies.

It's hard to believe that seasoned English troops would mistake a
line of raggedy villagers for an army. But another account of the legend says that this second force was made up of Templar Knights – a
sight which really would have sent the English packing.

There is no proof that either version is true. We do know, however,
that Robert the Bruce gave the Knights Templar protection in Scotland, created the Order of Heridom and the Brothers of the Rosy Cross
for them and gave them lands in Argyllshire. Pretty generous considering the rest of Europe was doing their utmost to wipe them out.

The Knights Templar are one of the many societies associated with
Edinburgh. Some are genuinely secretive – some are just little under-
stood because of public apathy. It's easy to find out about the
Company of Archers (the Sovereign's bodyguard in Scotland) or the
Order of the Thistle (a chivalric society with their own chapel in St

Giles). It just that not many people can be bothered and, anyway, both are fairly modern re-inventions of older societies.

Other sects deliberately keep a low profile, like the 'Monks of St Giles' - a gentleman's club who meet once a month in Candlemaker Row to wear monks' robes, drink and recite poetry. Few people in the city know they exist - but reciting poetry, no matter how outlandish your costume, is hardly a sinister secret.

Edinburgh does have a long history of covert orders, beginning with medieval city guilds such as the Hammermen and Goldsmiths, who zealously protected the skills of their craft from outsiders. Then, in the 18th century a whole plethora of strangely named societies sprang up - such as the Crochallan Fencibles (of which Robert Burns was a member) and the Marrow-bone club. Nut they were basically just drinking clubs who did military manoeuvres and discussed matters of the day. There were other, altogether less savoury, societies like the Knights of the Horn Order, The Atheisticall Club and The Jezebel Club – who revelled in the carnal, their ceremonies heavily influenced by Pagan and even Satanic rituals. The most high-profile was the Wig Club which was dedicated to sex and drinking and venerated a wig made from the pubic hair of Charles II's mistresses. Nice.

But being a secretive organization isn't the same as being a secret society. A truly secret society doesn't want you to know what they actually do or how much power they have.

Edinburgh has them too.

In December 2003 several national newspapers report an alleged cover up into the investigation of the Dunblane Massacre in 1996 – when Thomas Hamilton slaughtered sixteen children and one teacher then shot himself.

The investigation of the tragedy was headed by the Rt. Hon. Lord Cullen – Scotland's most senior judge. According to the *News of the World*, Hamilton had been a regular visitor at another school - the

Queen Victoria – which had long-standing links to high office. The Cullen inquiry failed to investigate claims of abuse at Queen Victoria School or the fact that Hamilton - a suspected paedophile – was allowed to freely wander around the school, run camps there and use the school shooting range. A *Sunday Herald* investigation found that documents pertaining to the cased had been ordered sealed for a century. The *Guardian* newspaper reported allegations that this lengthy closure order was placed on the reports after they linked Hamilton to senior legal and political figures in the Scottish establishment.

Lord Burton - a former grand master of the Masonic Society - sensationally claimed that there had been a cover up to protect high-profile legal figures. He stated these powerful men all belonged to the Edinburgh based 'Speculative Society'. Lord Cullen was also a member.

The Speculative Society was formed in 1764 as an offshoot of the Masons and has counted Sir Walter Scott, Robert Louis Stevenson and Hugh MacDiarmid among its most members. Its associates meet in candlelit vaults below Edinburgh University's Old College and its membership (which was secret until 2003) reads like a Who's Who of the rich and powerful in Scotland.

The Society was eventually investigated by ScoLAG (the Scottish Legal Action Group) – who concluded that the group was 'not a threat to democracy and justice'.

This is where the conspiracy theorists can have a field day - the greatest defence a secret society can have is to convince people they aren't a threat – and if anyone can pull a feat like that off, it's a society made up of the upper strata of Scotland's legal system.

Edinburgh strikes you as a city where surreptitious societies would flourish. Too many locked doors in dark alleys with no clue as to where they go. Buildings in hidden courtyards with no clue as to what they're for. Old clubs with rituals that involve dressing up in weird costumes.

But the city's two most controversial 'secret' societies are the most famous – oxymoronic as that may seem. The innuendo, misinformation, mythos and suspicion that surround these organisations has made them legendary.

The Masons and the Knights Templar

* * * *

Masonry may conjure up pictures of funny handshakes and men dancing round in moose antlers with their trousers rolled up – but the society of Freemasons has millions of members and is the oldest, largest, and most powerful fraternal order in the world. Despite this, they are still widely regarded as an insular and somewhat sinister group.

They were the most powerful of the 15th century worker's guilds and, unlike other tradesmen, could travel freely from country to country – earning them the obvious title of 'Freemasons'. The oldest surviving Masonic minutes in the world date from 1599 taken in Edinburgh and its oldest Masonic Lodge room still in use is Edinburgh's Canongate Kilwinning Lodge No. 2.

Scotland was an ideal place for the Masonic Society to flourish - the Scots continued to use crude stone as a building tool after other nations had turned to carved bricks and early in the seventeenth century, when Masonic unions across Europe began to decline, Scotland is credited with upholding the craft.

The most common form of Masonry is Craft Masonry where members complete three 'degrees' in order to become a Master Mason. (As with universities, a degree is attained after passing a Masonic exam). If they wish to go further, they can enter the more advanced 'Scottish Rite of Freemasonry' which includes degrees from the 4th to the 32nd. Scottish Rite Freemasonry originated in 18th century France, where large amounts of exiled Jacobites had fled from Scotland. Many of these expatriates were Masons and this 'Scottish' rite flourished in its new home.

Masons in Scotland wholeheartedly adopted its basic ideal that men are equal in moral worth rather than rank and station. In other countries, lodges became the exclusive preserve of 'accepted Masons' and tended to prohibit working men. In Scots lodges, noblemen and artisans could meet in lodges as brothers. Its philosophy had a great effect on the Edinburgh based Scottish Enlightenment. During that time Freemasonry was lauded as an organization promoting egalitarian views – policies which would eventually be adopted by both the revolutionary American and French governments. The poetry of Robert Burns is practically an advertisement for Masonic philosophy and he had intended to emigrate, until members of St John and the Canongate Kilwinning lodges got his first two volumes of poetry published.

But that seems to be the worst that Masons can be accused of - giving each other a hand up. You can be a Mason whether you are black, white or yellow, Christian, Muslim or Jew. What you can't be is an atheist or a woman – but believing the word 'equality' has a get-out clause doesn't make you evil, just misguided.

So does Freemasonry still have a dubious reputation – one that has rubbed off on Edinburgh?

Much of this suspicion comes from the Masonic association with the Knights Templar. Templars provided Freemasons with protection as they travelled about Europe and are reputed to have passed hidden knowledge on to them. The Masons also acquired the Templar's a reputation for secrecy – though the Order certainly had a good reason for keeping itself to itself.

* * * *

Over the centuries the Knights Templar have garnered a mythology that has reached epic proportions. To some the Order is a shining beacon of better times, while others consider it a long dormant coven of hidden evil. To most it is simply a mystery.

Accounts of the founding of the 'Poor Knights of Christ' are scant and sometimes contradictory. The generally accepted story is that they were a 12th century monastic military order formed by a lesser noble named Hughes De Payen to protect pilgrims on route to the Holy Land.

Within two centuries the Order had become much more than holy muscle for Christian travellers. Skirting round a papal law that forbad lending money with interest, they are credited with the invention of banking – to the point that they financed kings. This made them a huge threat as well as a huge asset. Even the Vatican – the only body they were answerable to – came to fear their power.

As the Templars drifted from their original goal as defenders of Christianity and settled into the role of powerbrokers in armour, the established orders in Europe began plotting to cut them down to size.

People didn't do things by halves in the Middle Ages and the assault on the Knights Templar was swift and ruthless. The Order was accused of heresy by the Vatican and charged with trampling on the cross, committing sodomy and worshiping a Devil named Baphomet. Their members were arrested, tortured and executed en masse - the last remaining Grand Master being burned at the stake in 1314. Their vast assets were seized by the financially strapped Philip of France – so it was easy to see why *he* wanted the Order out of the way.

Heresy was a pretty serious charge in 14th century Europe and nobody was going to defend the Templars against the combined might of the Roman Catholic Church and the Kingdom of France. The hapless Knights found themselves without allies and no country was willing to give them sanctuary. With one exception.

Scotland.

In Scotland, no order of suppression had been issued against the Templars as, under Scot's law, charges against the Order had been found 'Not Proven'. Other European monarchs weren't risking ex-communication for helping the Templars, but this was an empty threat against the Scots king. Robert the Bruce had already *been* excommunicated for murdering a rival on holy ground. Since then he had scored a gigantic military victory, won the crown of Scotland and gained independence for his country. For someone supposedly out of favour with God, Bruce was feeling pretty good about himself. Since he was locked in a war with England, France's deadly enemy, King Philip wasn't keen to penalise him either.

Shunned by the countries they had once protected, and with no chance of migrating east to Muslim lands, a large number of the Knights Templar fled to Scotland.

Not surprisingly the Order kept a low profile in their new home, but their influence was immediately felt - Templar rituals were even used at Bruce's burial. The Order set up their headquarters at Roslin, just outside Edinburgh and the St Clair (or Sinclair) family, owners of Roslin Castle, became its grand masters and cupbearers.

The Bruce line, and the Stuart dynasty that came after him, retained close ties to the Templars. In 1689, the Bonnie Dundee – who died defending the last Stuart king - was buried wearing the Grand Cross of the Order. Bonnie Prince Charlie was a senior Templar and on his doomed quest to regain the Stuart throne in 1745 he threw a soiree for the Chivalry of the Order in Holyrood Palace.

Perhaps he should have concentrated a little more on planning his campaign.

The Templars exist in Scotland today under the title *Militi Templi Scotia*. Their head is still the Sinclair family and their headquarters remains at Roslin. And they are still shrouded in mystery. You can take your pick of wild and wonderful Templar theories and Roslin is at the heart of all of them.

In fact, Roslin and the Sinclairs seem to be at the heart of a lot of things.

According to Scots lore there are legendary areas in this country known as 'Thin Places' – other countries have the same mythology under different names. A Thin Place is a location where this world and the world of the supernatural (or heaven or fairy land, or any other places we can't see or understand) are closest. Thin places are places of possibility, locations where the unusual is usual. The Island of Iona, where Christianity first took hold, has a reputation as a Thin Place. So does Balquhidder Glen, where Rob Roy Macgregor used to live.

And so does Roslin. It's a village, not even a town, yet it crops up again and again in Scottish history in the most remarkable ways. This place is the very stuff of myth.

Its first grand entrance on the stage of Scots history came in 1303, when the Scots and English clashed at the Battle of Roslin.

Let's be clear about Scottish/English conflicts. Scotland rarely won in any skirmish with the Auld Enemy – after a thousand years of fighting you can count our major victories on one hand, as long as you have six fingers. It wasn't through lack of courage, it was just that Scotland's fighters were never as well trained, well equipped, well fed or well led as their southern adversary. And they *certainly* didn't win when they were outnumbered.

To their credit the Scots, desperate for independence and led by the mighty William Wallace, had won the Battle of Stirling Bridge eight years earlier. But Wallace had then been crushed at the Battle of Falkirk, and Scottish hopes of freedom were dashed with him.

Yet the Battle of Roslin saw 8000 Scots annihilate an army of 30 000 English soldiers in the most decisive (as well as bloody) victory in Scottish history.

The battle actually came about because of a woman. The commander of the occupying forces in Edinburgh, John Seagrave, had become smitten by Margaret Ramsay of Dalhousie. The problem, apart from him being the enemy, was the fact that Margaret was engaged to Sir Henry Sinclair of Roslin. Forgoing the romantic approach, Seagrave gained permission from Edward of England to raise an army and attack Roslin. And Sinclair was waiting.

Place names at Roslin still bear witness to the massacre of the massive English force. Kilburn, Stinking Rig and Shinbanes Field commemorate the slaughter, the smell of corpses and the mass graves of the English.

The Scots had proved that they were not done yet. It would take another 12 years but at their next great battle – Bannockburn – Robert the Bruce would defeat another superior English force and secure Scottish freedom.

It was also the last major battle the Scots would ever win against England.

After Bannockburn, the Templars set up shop at Roslin Castle, with the Sinclairs becoming the grand masters of the Order. William de Sinclair even took Bruce's heart on a pilgrimage, since the king had never got round to going on one when he was alive. In 1330 Sinclair was killed defending the heart – which was saved and returned to Scotland. It is now buried in Melrose Abbey.

Henry Sinclair, son of William Sinclair, was born in Roslin Castle in 1345. At the age of 33 he was offered the title 'Earl of Orkney' and given the job of subduing these violent islands in the North of Scotland.

In the Orkneys he had heard tales of Mariners blown off course until they ended up at a huge land mass, far to the west. He brought in wood from Roslin, built and fitted out an expedition and headed in that direction.

Sinclair's fleet managed to cross the Atlantic without apparent loss, reached Nova Scotia and sailed down the coast of what is now

Massachusetts. He returned just as safely to Orkney in 1399 – almost a hundred years before Columbus 'discovered' the New World. What's more he actually landed on the mainland of North America - which Columbus never actually reached – and didn't mistake it for India when got there. He left proof of his journey in the shape of inscriptions in New England rocks and a 14th century cannon on Cape Breton Island.

Better still he left evidence in Roslin.

In 1444 Sinclair's grandson, William, built a beautiful chapel overlooking Roslin Glen – which still stands to this day. Inside are carvings of plants that do not correspond to any medieval interpretations of European flora. But they are easily recognisable to those familiar with indigenous American plants. They appear to be Maize and the effigies were carved half a century before Columbus.

Roslin Chapel is now famous the world over. It is widely believed that some great secret lies in the massive vaults under the ornate church, chambers which were sealed in 1690 and never reopened. According to lore, the hidden bargains in this secret basement range from Templar riches to Christ's Head, to the Holy Grail itself. Speculation is still rife as to what this ancient Order is actually hiding down there.

Here's my favourite. Behind the Templars are an even more super-secret society known as the Prieure de Sion (or Priory of Zion). They protect undiscovered accounts of Christ's life – including the proof that he had a son, was married to Mary Magdalene and wanted her to carry on his teachings. This would mean that the New Testament gospels are wrong and Christ was a mortal man who had descendants. And guess what Christ's descendants are allegedly called?

The Sinclairs.

Quite a lot for the Christian faith to accept, though it must give you a twinge of pleasure if Sinclair happens to be your second name.

The opposing camp insist that the Priory of Sion is a 20th century invention by a Frenchman named Pierre Plantard, who had been in prison for fraud and embezzlement - and that earlier documents pertaining to the Priory are fakes.

That's the problem with finding out the truth behind secret societies. Everything is such a big secret.

There are too many conflicting stories about Roslin's connections with the Templars, the Holy Grail, secret societies and the like to go into. A dozen books have been written about the subject from scholarly treatises to the best seller *The DaVinci Code*. It all goes to lending Roslin an unparalleled air of mystery.

Naturally, it has acquired a formidable haunted reputation – even Roslin Chapel – and it's very unusual for churches to have ghost stories.

Roslin Chapel is reputed to be haunted by an order of Augustine monks known as the Black Canons. The most reliable witness to these sightings was Judith Fiskin, the archivist and curator at Roslin during the 1980's. She also claimed to see the ghost of a Benedictine or Cistercian monk – this time with corroborating witnesses. Since then these apparitions have been witnessed several times.

The chapel is haunted by the ghost of a Mason's apprentice - credited in legend with creating the chapel's beautifully ornate 'Apprentice Pillar'. According to lore the, master Mason was so annoyed at the pillar being better than his attempts, he killed the craftsman.

The ruins of Roslin Castle, a few hundred yards away are haunted by a hound called the Mauthe Dog – slaughtered along with his English master at the battle of Roslin. There is also the obligatory white lady - Lady Bothwell, who was turned out of her home by Regent Moray in the late 16th century.

In recent centuries Roslin hasn't produced any major surprises, except for an ultra-sonic investigation into the chapel grounds which discovered there really are huge vaults down there. (Which are still sealed). But, if you really are a secret society working for an even more secret society, guarding one of the world's greatest secrets you don't want to draw too much attention to yourself.

However, a Thin Place will out in the end.

In 1997 the Roslin Institute, which had also been quietly going about its business for years, rocked the world by producing Dolly the Sheep – the world's first clone. There is no doubt that this is an achievement which fundamentally changed the world as we know it – both physically and spiritually.

This makes Roslin home to the most legendary religious order in history. It may be the place that holds proof of Christ's divinity. On the other hand, it could harbour the evidence for his mortality. And it is the site where man first got to play God.

That's irony on a cosmic scale

For that, Roslin gets my vote as a genuinely supernatural place and one that adds to Edinburgh's occult reputation no end.

Chapter 8

Spooky Books

Literature adds to reality, it does not simply describe it.

CS Lewis

The man in the frock coat and top hat stared at the cemetery gates. It was late and he had been walking for some time in an unfamiliar town, looking for a place just like this. He needed somewhere quiet and atmospheric to think, for he had a vague idea for a new book scratching at the corners of his mind. A different kind of book. An important book. But the story was eluding him.

The man pushed open the cemetery gate. It was not as dark inside as he had expected and a thin layer of Edinburgh's ever present fog lay across the lambent ground. A row of gas lamps cut the graveyard in two, bordering a narrow path that led downhill to the northern wall and lower gate opening onto the Cowgatehead. He ventured further into the cemetery, skirting gravestones, trying to discern bushes from shadows. The place was deserted. Taking off his hat he sat on a low wall and looked up at the stars. The church, a boxy Presbyterian monolith, was in the way. It reminded him of the one he used to worship in as a child.

There was a harsh cough to his left. The gentleman leapt to his feet, his top hat tumbling to the ground, heart pounding.

From behind a tall gravestone an old man emerged. Though his clothes were dirty and frayed, they had been carefully mended over and over and he held himself erect, his scrawny shoulders flung back. His stubbled face might have once been imposing but now it was gaunt and grey and his thinning hair pushed away from his head like wisps of factory smoke.

"Forgive me sir." The voice of the derelict man was rasping but his accent was not one of a commoner. "I wonder if you could spare a penny or two that I might purchase proper lodgings and perhaps a bath for one night." The old gent looked apologetically down at his shabby and soiled clothes. "I am not used to approaching strangers in this way, but judging by your own attire you seem a man of some means." He shrugged and tried a friendly smile. Two of his front teeth were broken.

The man in the frock coat liked to think himself a charitable sort. He had written essays in London arguing that fallen women should be rehabilitated rather than deported. He did not, however, take kindly to being accosted in the street – well, the graveyard - and panhandled in this way. He stared at the tramp, wondering how best to phrase his concerns and still avoid fisticuffs.

"It's not just for myself, you see." the old man said suddenly. "I have companions who have also experienced the... darker side of life, shall we say."

And there they were. Drifting towards him out of the darkness. A huge man with a matted black beard. A little boy and girl, painfully thin – their dead eyes revealing nothing but incomprehension and hunger. A small fellow, his hands twisted into claws, whether by ill heath, bad breeding or some terrible accident it was impossible to tell.

The man in the frock coat took an involuntary step back. the hairs rising on the back of his neck. But he was a fellow of principles and refused to be weak in his convictions or feeble in his mannerisms. He stared at the ragged group, standing knee deep in the mist.

Behind them, on the other side of the graveyard wall, he could see the thick minarets of Herriot's Orphanage, erected by the great Victorian philanthropist. To his left, equally close, the workhouse with its dormitories and kitchens was also visible. Beyond that was the Bedlam asylum, overseen by the doctors of Edinburgh – and this city cultivated some of the finest legal minds in the world.

What more could these wretches expect from a society that was prepared to look after them so?

The man's gaze hardened. He swept his top hat out of the murk and grimly shook his head. The children's' eyes brightened with hatred and the giant started forward with a bitter grin, the glint of a small knife in his hand.

His older companion raised a restraining arm.

"No. Let the Topper go," he said sadly. "We will show him more charity than he has given us."

And they slowly retreated, until shadows, mist, gravestones and the night had merged together to envelop them all.

The man in the frock coat walked unsteadily back to the entrance. He was shaking too badly to immediately present himself on the street, so he sat down on a flat tombstone near the entrance. He had been badly frightened by the experience and, for a moment, thought he was going to die. And it was true - in a situation so grave a man's whole existence flashed before his eyes. For a second, he had believed the greater things he hoped to achieve would never happen. How horrible to have one's life end when it was not fully lived! In a nearby tree an owl hooted. A startled cat raced from the bushes and snaked along the base of the wall. The man removed his hat again, took a deep quavering breath, and lowered his head into his hands.

Through his spread fingers he caught sight of the inscription on the tombstone next to him. His eyes narrowed. The darkness made it hard to read the words and he had to bring his face so close to the rough stone that he felt its coldness.

Surely the inscription couldn't be right. And yet... he was reading it with his own eyes

Ebeneezer Scroggie. Mean man

The man in the frock coat sat back, horrified. What kind of creature would be given an epitaph like that? Who could be so despised that even his last resting place proclaimed him a rogue and a miser? He got unsteadily to his feet and, glancing one more time at the tomb, staggered from the graveyard.

As he left that place of death, destitution and loneliness, and stepped out into the streetlights, he felt as if a great weight had been lifted from his soul. On impulse he gave a quiet little dance, no more than a shuffle really - a gentleman remained a gentleman at all times.

Across the street, at the top of Candlemaker Row, a little boy was watching with wistful curiosity. Or maybe he just thought the man in the top hat was insane. The child leaned heavily to one side, a home made ash crutch tucked under his skinny oxter.

The gentleman raised an arm in greeting and strode over to him. The boy flinched. The man shook his head kindly and bent down until they were level.

"What's your name, boy?" he said softly.

The lad looked at him timidly. "Tim, sir."

The gentleman fished in his pocket and pulled out a pound note. The boy's eyes widened in astonishment as the money was pressed into his small calloused hand. The gentleman winked.

"Merry Christmas, Tim."

The boy gave a small choking sound. The toff was obviously drunk or a loon, and he didn't want to get into trouble.

"Beggin pardon sir," he said, gazing longingly at the money in his palm. "It's the middle of July."

The man looked back the way he had come. Fog still covered the graveyard floor, thick as undisturbed snow, vanishing into the darkness like a fairy tale. On top of the high iron gate was a small gas lamp that cast a spectral yellow pall across the entrance. It matched the cheerful glow emanating from the windows of Greyfriars Inn next door. He glanced through the thick whorls of glass at the distorted almost caricatured faces. Patrons were joking and drinking and slapping each other's backs. Laughter drifted out of the door and he heard a rough Scots voice cry out a toast, a drunken variation on the famous words of Robert Burns.

"Good cheer tae us and God bless us, everyone."

Charles Dickens gave a smile and patted the boy on the arm.

"Yes. God bless us one and all," he said.

He tilted his hat at a jaunty angle and set off down the street.

In fact, Dickens, on a short visit to an Edinburgh cemetery, had read the tombstone incorrectly. It actually said *Ebeneezer Scroggie: Meal man.*

The poor bloke was a corn dealer in the city.

But the rest is history. Two years later Charles Dickens completed the book *A Christmas Carol.* Not only did it give the world a superb villain in Ebeneezer Scrooge, but a classic supernatural trio in the ghosts of Christmas Past, Present and Future. Despite the happy ending, it is one of the greatest and most chilling Victorian horror novels.

But it's not the only one that this city inspired.

Edinburgh has played a role in numerous literary achievements, not just within the horror genre. Europe's great fount of secular knowledge, *The Encyclopaedia Britannica* was compiled, edited and printed in the city. Its most widely read spiritual work – *The King James Bible* – was commissioned and supervised by James VI. Over the years the city has been the residence or birthplace of a host of famous and acclaimed authors. Oh, and me as well.

Allan Ramsay, Norman MacCaig, Daniel Defoe, David Hume, Adam Smith, Thomas Carlyle, Hugh MacDairmid, Robert Burns, Sir Walter Scott, Percy Shelley, Robert Fergusson, R M Ballantyne, J M Barrie, R L Stevenson, Kenneth Grahame, Muriel Spark, Compton Mackenzie, Liz Lockhead, Ian Banks, Ian Rankin, Anita Sullivan, Brookmyer, Quentin Jardine, James Robertson and Irvine Welsh – to name but a few - have all rubbed literary shoulders in the narrow streets of this city.

Admittedly, there's nothing scary about that, unless you actually bump into Irvine Welsh in a narrow street. But Edinburgh has black, black ink in some of its pens and they have left an indelible mark on the pages of time.

This city has links to more famous literary monsters than you could fit under a bunk bed.

Edinburgh's more sinister influences first came to the public's attention through a spate of 16th and 17th century books about the supernatural. The Mercat cross on the Royal Mile, for instance, is famous as the site where the Devil predicted the battle of Flodden. This is because the incident was recounted in Robert Lindsay's *Historie and Chronicles of Scotland*. Bear in mind that this was a history book, not a work of fiction – the appearance of Auld Nick in the centre of Edinburgh was presented as an unquestioned fact. Other 'serious' works, like Reverend Robert Law's *The Memorable Things that Fell Out within this Island of Brittain from 1638 to 1684* also pointed an accusing finger towards Edinburgh being the capital of weird.

Of course you can't get worse press than being written about by your own king – especially when he was born in the place. As well as overseeing the Bible, James IV personally wrote *Demonology* in 1597 – just in case the good book wasn't going to be specific enough on the Satanic problem. The fact that he thought the witches of Edinburgh and neighbouring North Berwick were out to get him didn't exactly put a halo over the city. Things were made worse when, in 1591, *Newes From Scotland* – published in London - gave a graphic and widely read account of the monarch's battle with the same Satanic henchmen.

Richard Bovet's *Pandæmonium, or the Devil's Cloister Opened* (1683) described vividly the story of the Fairy Boy of Leith and Professor George Sinclair portrayed Edinburgh as a hotbed of supernatural activity in his 1685 bestseller, *Satan's Invisible World Discovered*. This book in particular went through many editions and would have formed part of nearly any library in Scotland. The full title *Satan's Invisible World Discovered or A Choice Collection of Modern Revelations, Proving Evidently, Against the Atheists of this Present Age, that there are Devils, Spirits, Witches and Apparitions.* This wasn't just a collection of entertaining ghostly tales - It was a warning. The good professor was determined to tell it like it was.

Nathaniel Crouch, in *The Kingdom of Darkness* (1688) exposed Sinclair's stories to an even larger audience - these books cementing Edinburgh's reputation as the creepy capital of a decidedly paranormal country. They made a celebrity of Major Weir and turned Mary Kings Close (see MKC) into phenomenon. It's a measure of their influence that Weir has remained famous and Mary Kings Close is still considered to be one of the world's most haunted locations.

After that, all the great Edinburgh writers had to have a go at horror – even if it wasn't their preferred genre. Robert Burns, who lived in Lady Stairs Close, wrote ditties about ghosts and Satan and his most famous work is *Tam O Shanter* - the poem, of course, concerning a drunken race against a coven of witches. His equally talented contemporary, Robert Fergusson wrote spooky poetry too, including one about Greyfriars Churchyard, *The Ghaists: A Kirkyard Epilogue*

Cauld blaws the nippin north wi angry south
And showers his hailstanes frae the Castle Cleugh
Owr the Greyfriars, whare at mirkest hour
Bogles and spectres wont to take their tour

Ironically, he died at the age of 24 in the Bedlam Asylum, just out-side the graveyard gates, after falling down a flight of stairs.

Edinburgh has produced some of the most famous writers in the world – and they've all enhanced its sinister reputation by having a go at writing creepy stories.

Walter Scott is a prime example. It is almost impossible to under-estimate his influence and, appropriately, he has the largest monument to a writer on the planet – the Scott monument on Princes Street. Once the most famous man in Europe, he had a truly astounding talent for re-invention. He transformed the cold and brutal highlands into a heather covered paradise stocked with noble warriors in books like *Rob Roy* and *Redgauntlet* – a perception that persists to this day. His writings about America prompted a blistering attack from Mark Twain – who more or less accused Scott of starting the American Civil War.

Sir Walter had so large a hand in making Southern character, as it existed before the war, that he is in great measure responsible for the war.

Scott 'found' the Scottish crown Jewels which had been missing for almost a century – now on display in Edinburgh castle. He organ-ised a visit to Edinburgh by George IV in 1822 and got a mass of highland clans to descend on Edinburgh – the first time it had ever happened without a major bloodbath. He invented a national dress for them – including most of the tartans we have today (Yes, *that's* how they came about) and the lowlanders liked their kilts so much that they all got one too. In August 1822, for the first time *in its history* Scot-land was an undivided nation. Walter Scott altered the way this country saw itself and, in doing so, altered the world's perception of Scotland too.

This is myth making on a colossal scale – nothing else in history has ever come close. But Scott knew that his 'Edinburgh Pageant' had just thrown a nice tartan shawl over a dark metropolis. He had a life-long interest in the supernatural and freely admitted encountering apparitions. His first poems were included in *An Apology for Tales of Terror* (1799), his first book *Minstrelsy of the Scottish Borders* (1802) was a collection of supernatural ballads and short horror stories like *The Tapestried Chamber* and *My Aunt Margaret's Mirror* are considered classics to this day. It wasn't until 1830 that he wrote a sceptical account of the persecution of so called witches - *Letters On Demonology and Witchcraft*. As soon as it was published, he was attacked by the *Edinburgh Literary Journal*, who derided his 'lack of depth' in researching his theory of supernatural visitations.

None of this did anything to lessen the perception of his city as a ghost town.

In 1810 a young man named John Polidori enrolled at Edinburgh University Medical Department, next to Greyfriars Graveyard. This was at the height of the city's body snatching period – a time when enterprising fellows dug up fresh corpses and sold them to the university's Anatomy department to experiment on.

Six years later, Polidori found himself at Villa Diodoti on the shores of Lake Geneva, along with the writers Lord Byron, Percy Shelly's and Shelly's wife, Mary. Freaking each other out by reading horror stories, they decided to see if they could do better themselves.

It's somehow satisfying that Shelly and Byron – the two arch egoists – didn't come up with anything much at all. But Polidori wrote The *Vampyr* – which features a dentally challenged aristocratic and is generally regarded to be the world's first 'proper' vampire story. It's easy to work out which famous gothic novel *that* inspired. There is no evidence that Bram Stoker based Count Dracula on Vlad the Impaler, or even knew about some obscure, Wallachian voivode. But he read Poldori's story and chunks of his gothic masterpiece *were* written in Scotland.

Polidori was on a roll that night for he helped inspire yet another famous horror tome. During an evening of telling horror stories, it seems certain the medical man would have mentioned Edinburgh's body snatchers – and his tales would have been corroborated by Percy Shelly, who was in the capital around the same time. Polidori would have also known of experiments at Edinburgh University into 'Medical Electricity' – in which anatomists tried to bring back corpses from the dead by running live currents through them.

Lo and behold, Mary Shelly then begins writing *Frankenstein* - the story of a medical man who steals corpses and tries to bring them back to life. She may well have been familiar with these stories anyway – she grew up outside Dundee, a mere 60 miles from Edinburgh

1824 saw the publication of Edinburgh resident James Hogg's *Confessions of a Justified Sinner* – set in the city. It is the first book to deal with either Satanic possession or schizophrenia, depending on how you look at it.

At the same time, the Victorian essayist Hugh Millar was writing widely read tracts on the paranormal. Although a famous scientist, he believed firmly in all things spooky and committed suicide in Portobello because of paranoid delusions about being hounded by an invisible entity.

Or perhaps he really was being hounded by an invisible entity.

In 1831 Edinburgh author Leith Ritchie wrote *The Man Wolf* – one of the first ever werewolf stories.

In 1843 Charles Dickens brought out *A Christmas Carol*.

In 1886 an Edinburgh author came up with what is arguably the greatest horror story ever published. As well as writing popular short horror stories, Robert Louis Stevenson's *Dr Jekyll and Mr Hyde* was a masterpiece that had a profound effect on the way the human race saw itself – anticipating the works of Freud and Jung by decades. It was inspired by the duplicitous life of local villain Deacon William Brodie but in many ways I think it is about Edinburgh itself – a city about whose internal divisions Stevenson often wrote passionately.

Another giant of gothic fiction was born the same year as Mr Hyde - Sherlock Holmes. Arthur Conan Doyle was another city writer who went to the University Medical School near Greyfriars and he based Holmes partly on an Edinburgh doctor named Joseph Bell. Holmes' arch enemy Moriarty is inspired by yet *another* medical student at Edinburgh University – a serial killer named Thomas Cream.

It is true that both Holmes and Hyde stalked the misty streets of Victorian London, but the fact that both authors were from Edinburgh gave their home city an equally sinister gravitas in the minds of the public.

Conan Doyle was also Britain's foremost champion of Spiritualism - a 19th century movement began by the Fox family in New York, who claimed they could communicate with the spirits. Sceptics suspected these 'mediums' were fraudsters but the spiritualist movement grew rapidly into an organized religion which flourishes today. For someone whose most famous creation lived by the value of logic and deduction, Conan Doyle was much more a Watson than a Holmes. Even when one of the Fox sisters confessed to being a fraud, he refused to believe it.

He was also convinced of the existence in Fairies and defended this quaint but far-fetched notion vigorously in print.

Or perhaps he wrote from experience. Doyle was born in the shadow of Calton Hill – legendary as a fairy den.

A footnote to all this. Conan Doyle famously described Professor Moriarity as the 'Napoleon of Crime'. This is also the description T.S. Elliot gave to the feline villain *Macavity the Mystery Cat* in *Old Possum's Book of Practical Cats.* The cats were allegedly based on real moggies he had observed on a 1937 visit to Greyfriars. (If you don't think that's got anything to do with horror, go and see the musical *Cats*.)

The fantasy/horror connection to Greyfriars Graveyard doesn't end there. J.K. Rowling wrote *Harry Potter and the Philosophers Stone* in a café window overlooking the cemetery. If you look across the view you can see Heriot's School – the huge castle-like building that was once an orphanage. I used to write overlooking the graveyard too. Hey, it's my only chance to stick myself in the same paragraph as J.K. Rowling and I can't resist it.

Of all the books that celebrate the city's occult side, my favourite is *The Key to World History* by Comyns Beaumont, published in 1948. It puts forward the astonishing theory that the biblical depictions of Jerusalem are actually talking about Edinburgh and he argues this mind boggling point rather eloquently. All right, it still sounds crazy, but Beaumont's eccentric theories have been proved right before. He was the originator of the 'Catastrophe Theory' – the idea that earth's history was periodically altered by cataclysmic collisions with comets. The hypothesis was scoffed at when he first wrote it, but we now know it to be correct – it's how the dinosaurs died out, for a start.

He was the first man to explain anomalies in Old Testament timelines by suggesting that the Egyptian Calendar was inaccurate. He also claimed that Venus once had an erratic orbit which brought it close enough to earth to cause ruinous damage to early civilizations. After decades of protest, both theories are finally gaining credence among scientists.

So, you never know.

Today Edinburgh has a new school of famous writers, whose plots are as dark and twisty as Satan's knitting. Ian Bank's *The Wasp Factory* is one of the creepiest things I have ever read. Irvine Welsh with *Trainspotting,* Ian Rankin with the Rebus novels, Quentin Jardine's *Skinner* series and Christopher Brookmyer's *Quite Ugly one Morning* positively revel in the malicious side of Edinburgh. Jonathan Aycliffe's Faustian chillier *The Matrix* and James Robertson's *The Fanatic* portray Edinburgh as a malevolent entity lurking under a thin veneer of sophistication.

Even Batman recognises this. In Alan Grant's *Batman: The Scottish Connection*, the caped crusader swaps Gotham City to seek out evil in Scotland's capital - and he looks just right crouching on the misty ramparts of the Castle. Fittingly, he also gets mixed up with the Knights Templar at Roslin.

Holy Grail, Batman!

There can be no doubt that a great part of this city's sinister reputation has come from literary associations and accusations. And physical reminders of what was written still pack the city. The places where witches, heretics, Covenanters and criminals were executed are still there. Greyfriars is unchanged. So is St Giles' Cathedral. The Mercat Cross still stands, even if it has been moved a little. The Old Town at night looks as ancient and ominous as ever. Stroll through the Georgian and Victorian New Town and you can almost see Henry Jekyll doffing his top hat at a handsome cab. Edinburgh may have ranked second to London as the ultimate fog bound edifice, but is crammed with narrow alleys where any number of unnamed horrors might lurk. Its big advantage in the creepy stakes is that London has changed beyond recognition. This city hasn't.

That can leave a disturbing impression in the minds of people who visit. If it still *looks* like the setting for hidden horrors – perhaps it still *is*.

Admittedly, many of the literary works mentioned here are fictional and the non-fiction ones have a credibility gap as wide as the river Styx. I suppose it's possible that the Devil *did* appear on the steps of the Mercat Cross – Edinburgh is a tourist town after all. But he doesn't seem to have been impressed enough to make a second trip.

As far as proof goes, the ghosts of Edinburgh's past may as well be as fictional as Dickens's Christmas ones. Witnesses are long gone and a vast percentage of sightings were reported in centuries when the existence of the supernatural simply wasn't questioned.

In a sense all writing is propaganda - and spooky propaganda has done as much for Edinburgh's haunted status as any real ghost. Which leads us to the most pragmatic reason why this city has a haunted reputation.

It wants one.

Chapter 9

Very Bad Things

Tourist interest in recent deaths, disaster and atrocity is a growing phenomenon

Professor John Lennon

Three men stood in the shadows of the Excise office in Chessels Court, hugging the thick shadows at the base of the towering tenements. A fourth, Andrew Ainslie, was at the entrance to the alleyway keeping watch. The close was as narrow and dirty as any other in the Old Town - but at three in the morning it was deserted, except for a few scavenging rats and cats. In the darkness it was hard to tell which was which.

Smith was dancing around kicking at vermin and household pets indiscriminately.

"Will you put your bloody mask on?" Deacon Brodie couldn't hide his irritation. He had a bad feeling about this particular raid – but the Excise Office was his passport to a fortune. He couldn't turn back now.

"I can't see properly," Smith grunted sulkily. "I think I cut the eyeholes in the wrong place."

Brodie sighed. Behind him he heard a soft burp. Humphry Moore was leaning against the wall – a black cloth wrapped round his face, red rimmed eyes peering from two slashed slits.

"Have you been drinking?"

"Why certainly not Mr Brodie, sir. I had a couple of mugs of ale in the Anchor Bar, just to be sociable, you know." Moore slid a little further down the wall. "And half a bottle of whisky to keep out the cold."

The Deacon turned away with a snort. Putting a cautionary finger to his lips, he produced a ring of keys from his pocket and fitted one in the large wooden door.

"Hadn't we better knock first, just in case there's someone in-side?" Smith had succeeded in ripping a larger hole in his mask. Now both eyes poked through, as well as his nose and one ear.

"My sources have assured me that the place is empty," Brodie countered. "And if anyone was inside, one sniff of Moore's breath would knock them out."

"How did you get the key anyways?"

"I'm a town councillor as well as a locksmith," replied the Deacon haughtily. "If I chose, I could break into Holyrood Palace itself." He gently turned the key and there was a soft click. One push and the door swung slowly open.

"Silence is the real key lads," he said with a wink. Moore pried himself away from the wall and fell over a pile of wooden crates. With another sigh, Brodie hauled him to his feet and pushed the giggling man inside. Smith shoved the door closed behind them.

"The safe used by the tax office is on the top floor. We can't use lights or someone outside might see. But I've been here a dozen times. Memorised the layout." Brodie turned and walked into a coat stand.

"Maybe they moved that, sir," Moore said understandingly. Brodie gave him a slap on the back of the head.

They made their way slowly up the four flights of stairs to the top of the building, stopping every now and then to let Smith pull up his mask.

"I never was very good at knots," he complained. Eventually Brodie tied it at the back for him.

At last they reached the top landing and let themselves into the Excise Office. The safe was a large solid square in the corner of the room. Deacon Brodie fished out another key, inserted it and pulled the bulky iron door open. He knelt down, pulled the contents onto the floor and inspected them.

"How much is there?"

There was a silence from the crouched figure on the floor.

"I'm going to buy buckles for my shoes as big as dogs," Moore confided dreamily. "And I'll get my feet treated. I have terrible warty toes, you know."

Smith bent down beside his leader.

"How much is there?"

"You want me to count it now?"

"It doesn't look like a big pile."

Brodie nodded in agreement. He flicked quickly through the large notes. There was another silence.

"Well. How much?"

"Eh.... Sixteen pounds."

"Excellent!" Moore chimed in. "How much is that split three ways?"

"Sixteen pounds!" Smith glared at the Deacon.

Brodie gave an embarrassed shrug. "My informant said the safe was full of money."

"Is this the same informant who said there wouldn't be anyone else in the building?"

Brodie nodded.

"Then I suggest we get the hell out of here."

The door opened and a bolt of yellow light cut through the room. In the doorway stood a tall figure in a cocked hat, lantern in one hand.

"And just what is going on here?" he inquired.

Smith sprang to his feet. "Leave this to me," he whispered to the stunned Deacon. He advanced on the stranger drawing himself to his full height of five foot four.

"My good man," he said forcefully. "Don't you know who you're talking to? Why this is Deacon Brodie, a respected town councillor. He's on official business."

"Shut up you idiot!" Brodie hissed. "We're wearing masks."

"Oh. Sorry."

Suddenly Moore rushed drunkenly past them, catching the intruder round the midriff. Both men vanished out of the doorway and the other robbers could hear them bouncing down the stairs.

"It's all right now, Mr Brodie, sir." A shaky voice floated out of the darkness below. "Thank God I was inebriated or I might have broken my neck."

Brodie grabbed the money and he and Smith thundered down the darkened stairs. Moore was upside down on the second landing next to the unconscious stranger. Hauling their accomplice to his feet they manhandled him into the alleyway and locked the door behind them.

Ainslie was still crouched at the entrance to the close, beckoning frantically. Brodie strode over to him, his face grim.

"I thought I told you to whistle if a night watchman came along," he fumed.

"It wasn't a night watchman. It was the Deputy Solicitor of Excise."

"Why didn't you do something?"

Ainslie frowned. "I did. I hid behind that barrel."

"Rich beyond our wildest dreams." Moore gave a contented burp and fell over the crates again. Deacon Brodie gave him one last slap and headed up the Royal Mile.

Deacon William Brodie is one of Edinburgh's most famous sons. He was indeed a town councillor and a wealthy man, but he was also a gambler, who lost vast amounts of money on cock fights. It might not have been such a problem if he hadn't three families to support – his own and one from each of his two mistresses.

To supplement his lifestyle he took up burglary, and given his respectable position, it wasn't difficult for him to gain access to most dwellings. But the hauls he had gotten away with just weren't large enough, so he decided to enlist the help of accomplices on his largest escapade. When he attempted to rob the Edinburgh Excise office in Chessels court on March 5th 1788, he took with him George Smith, Andrew Ainslie and Humphry Moore.

The robbery was a fiasco – and one of his accomplices had a dark secret that was to doom the Deacon. Humphrey Moore, alias John Brown, was a wanted man in England and knew that if he was caught for this robbery he would be deported. On the other hand, if he turned informer, he would be called as a witness. And he wouldn't be admissible as a witness unless pardoned for his crimes in England.

He was sorted. Knowing the Edinburgh authorities would rather catch a big fish than deport a small one he promptly turned himself in. Smith and Ainslie were arrested and Brodie fled to Amsterdam where he intended to book passage to America.

But Brodie was no criminal mastermind. Posing as 'John Dixon' he gave a fellow traveller named Geddes a pile of goodbye letters to take back to Edinburgh – including one to his mistress. Geddes worked out the true identity of John Dixon, contacted the authorities, and Brodie was arrested in Amsterdam.

By this time Ainslie had also confessed to the authorities and, on Oct 1, 1788, Smith and Brodie were hung for the Excise Office robbery. Ironically Brodie himself had designed the mechanism for the new gallows

Deacon Brodie may have been a cad in life but he faced death in a much more heroic manner. On the scaffold he chatted casually with his friends. When the drop had to be delayed twice due to technical difficulties Brodie wittily remarked. "After all, one has to get used to these new contraptions."

Talk about gallows humour.

Macabre legends sprang up around him from the instant of his death - in this case quite literally.

It is said there was a plot to rescue Brodie at the last minute but the vast crowd and the soldiers called in to keep order made this impossible.

It is said that a French quack tried to revive him, without success. Brodie had requested that his body had been handed over to his friends and no sooner was this done then they vanished with it – presumably to attempt the resuscitation.

It is said that Brodie's friends had sneaked him a silver tube, which he put down his throat to prevent strangulation – it's also said that he ended up choking to death on it.

With all those safeguards in place, no wonder the man was nonchalant about his fate. Shame none of them actually worked.

Or did they?

It is said that when his tomb was opened some time later, the coffin was empty. There's no way to prove it, of course. It's almost certain that he did die but his burial site is long gone, so we will never know.

Then again there are no ghost stories in Edinburgh involving Deacon Brodie, which is unusual considering all the legends he inspired.

So maybe he made it after all.

Regardless of the man's ultimate fate, the story of Deacon Brodie was too good to die. When Robert Louis Stevenson based the fictional characters Dr Jekyll and Mr Hyde partly on the Deacon, he assured Brodie's name would live on forever.

In legends whenever good versus evil, good usually triumphs, right?

Not in Edinburgh.

I went out on the streets and did a little survey. I asked people if they had heard of Deacon Brodie. Most of them had, including many from other countries. Then I asked if they had heard of the Scottish Enlightenment. Most knew the term, but few had more than a rough idea of the details. A handful said (correctly) that it was a time when a lot of very smart people lived in Edinburgh, earning it the nickname 'The Athens of the North'.

Those were usually visitors to the city.

Not one person realised that this Edinburgh led movement altered the world as profoundly as the Italian Renaissance or the Reformation. That in the 18th century a sparkling concentration of scientists, artists and thinkers in this city revolutionized the literature, sociology, transport, communications, medicine and economics of the entire western world. That they were instrumental in the creation of modern Canada, Australia, Russia and Japan. That without them there would have been no American Revolution, Constitution or Dream. No British Empire, either.

It's hard to believe that now - today we couldn't even construct our own parliament building and tram system on time or budget.

I also asked my victims, I mean test subjects, a little quiz. *Spot the Edinburgh Genius.* I invited them to give me the names of local over-achievers based on a list of their accomplishments.

Try it at home with your loved ones if you like.

1. He is regarded as perhaps the greatest thinker the English speaking world has ever produced. He also came up with the theory of Causation.

David Hume.

2. His tireless human rights work in the 19th century made him the saviour of the Australian aborigines

Charles Sievwright.

3. He sent a wireless transmission a year before Marconi's famous 'discovery' of wireless

John Muirhead.

4. He realised bacteria caused disease and was treating it two decades before Louis Pasteur was officially credited with the discovery.

Dr John Goodsir

5. He wrote a book called *The Origin of Language*, containing a theory of evolution, a century before Charles Darwin's *Origin of the Species*.

James Burnett

6. He is regarded as the 'Father of Modern Geology' - correctly theorizing how the earth was formed then providing proof of its rotation.

James Hutton

7. He invented chloroform and was the first person to use anaesthesia in childbirth.

James Young Simpson

8. Arguably the greatest civil engineer of all time, he turned Scotland into the world leader in construction and introduced the concept of contractors.

Thomas Telford

9. He changed the world forever by introducing it to his theory of Capitalism

Adam Smith

10. He began the European Romantic movement in the 18th century and was once the most widely read writer on the continent.

James McPherson

12. He identified Carbon Monoxide, came up with the Theory of Combustion, discovered specific heat and introduced the manufacture of writing paper.

Joseph Black

13. He developed the Kinetic theory of gases, founded the science of statistical mechanics, originated the concepts of cybernetics, came up with the theory of electromagnetism, produced the theory of colour blindness and took the first colour photograph. He is regarded in the scientific community as being on a par with Einstein – who called his work "the most fruitful that physics has experienced since the time of Newton".

James Clerk Maxwell

14. He produced the world's first clone

Ian Wilmut

15. He started Britain's fist fire department in Edinburgh and went on to found the London Fire brigade.

James Braidwood

James Braidwood is a perfect example of how Edinburgh treats its heroes. In London there are streets named after him and monuments dedicated to the man. In Edinburgh he had one pub named after him – which then changed its name to the *Fire Station.* And is now called *Dragonfly.* He now has a statue in Parliament Square but nobody knows who it is.

Adam Smith – whose impact on the world is as great as any human who ever lived – finally got a statue in 2010. Before that he only had a badly tended grave in Canongate Churchyard. Hutton fares no better – there's a little plaque over his grave in Greyfriars. Burnett, also buried there, doesn't even have a headstone. Not one Edinburgh resident I asked had even heard of Sievwright, Muirhead, Goodsir, McPherson, Maxwell or Black.

David Hume does have one statue on the Royal Mile. It was erected in 1996 – almost three centuries after he was born. And he's wearing a toga.

On the other hand, take an Edinburgh character like Deacon Brodie. He is commemorated by a large pub on the Royal Mile and there is a Brodies café in Brodie's close across the street, with his effigy outside. He is famous as the inspiration for Dr Jekyll and Mr Hyde and a motion picture was made about his life.

Everybody in Edinburgh knows about the mass murderers Burke and Hare. They can tell you that Adam Lyall was a highwayman and that Maggie Dixon killed her own child. In previous centuries the criminal fraternity used to spit at the Tolbooth prison on the Royal Mile. A heart now marks the spot and that same tradition is rigorously carried out.

Why? Is Edinburgh's dark past so much more fascinating than its miraculous achievements?

In a word, yes. That's why I'm writing about it. The accomplishments of this city's great men are epic in scope and profound in their breadth and depth. But Deacon Brodie makes for a much better story.

He's not the only one. More famous than many of Edinburgh's most eminent citizen are the mass murderers William Burke and William Hare – though their dubious achievements are irrevocably tied to Edinburgh's scientific achievements, if that's any consolation.

William Burke and William Hare were Irish immigrants. In 1827 Burke settled in Edinburgh with his common law wife, where he became acquainted with William Hare and his spouse – who kept a cheap lodging house in Tanners Close, West Port.

In December a lodger died in the house and the two men saw an opportunity to turn this unfortunate incident into cash. At the time, Edinburgh University had the finest anatomy department in the world, with dozens of students eager to learn the practicalities of their profession. What they didn't have was bodies. And so a surreptitious trade in death was going on. 'Resurrection Men' would sneak into Edinburgh's graveyards at night and steal fresh corpses, which they would then sell under the dissecting table to the university.

And now Burke and Hare had a fresh corpse, without having to go to the trouble and danger of digging it up. So they sold the body to the anatomist Dr Knox for 7 pounds 10 shillings. And that gave them a great idea. It would save them all kinds of time and effort if they cut out the middle man and produced the corpses themselves.

So they began killing people.

They would invite drunk or derelict strangers to Hare's lodging house, get them even more inebriated, then Burke would suffocate them by ramming his fingers up the victim's nose. It's a method of killing known to this day in medical circles as 'Burking'.

In a 16 month period Burke and Hare killed sixteen people, before another lodger discovered a body under Hare's bed, ready to be delivered to Dr Knox. Burke, Hare and their spouses were subsequently arrested.

Hare immediately turned king's evidence and Burke went to trial alone. Imminent death seemed to bring out a long hidden decent streak in the murderer and his defence revolved around proving his wife had nothing to do with the crimes. He was executed on Wednesday 28th January 1829, and it was estimated that there were between thirty-two and forty thousand people turned up to see him die. They certainly knew how to entertain themselves in the old days. Ironically, the body was then taken to Edinburgh University and dissected.

There was no way Hare could be set free in the city, as the Edinburgh mob would have torn him to pieces, so he was put on a mail coach to London using the appropriate name of Mr Black. There are rumours that he was blinded and spent the rest of his life as a beggar – but there is no official record of what finally happened to him. The wives of the deadly pair also faded into obscurity.

You can still see a bit of Burke though! A book made out of his skin is on display in the Witchery Tour shop on the West Bow. And, continuing the skin theme, there's a lap dancing bar next to where he lived - the *Burke and Hare*.

But all cities have their villains. Why does Edinburgh push its grisly past on visitors with such relish?

To a great extent the answer is, it's good for business. There has been a rise in a phenomenon known as Dark Tourism – a term that Professors John Lennon and Malcolm Foley coined in their book *Dark Tourism: The attraction of Death and Disaster.* According to the professors, there is an unprecedented fascination with the dark and grisly side of history. As Glasgow's Caledonian Centre for Tourism research so tastefully put it.

Gone are the days when a nice holiday amounted to chargrilled families traipsing round Roman ruins wondering when Johnny Foreigner was going to get the place finished

For the record, I find Dark Tourism a ridiculous concept. All history is dark and grisly and comparing Auschwitz to ghost tours is truly offensive. But if you are looking for the darkest, most gruesome aspects of history – especially if you want physical evidence of that past - Edinburgh is the perfect city for you.

In the middle of the Royal Mile you can stand on the 'Heart of Midlothian' – a pavement memorial to notorious Tolbooth prison. I wouldn't though - it's usually covered in mucus, as people spit on it as a sign of disrespect. A few feet away are brass cobbles marking the site of the execution spots. A little further on is Deacon Brodie's Close and pub. Turn the other way and there is St Giles Cathedral – containing 'Haddo's Hole' - where Covenanters were held before being executed. It also held a guillotine, ready to be wheeled outside when needed. Next to that is the Mercat Cross, where debtors were put in stocks or had their ears nailed to wood. Both Mercat and City of the Dead ghost tours begin here and, across the road is Mary Kings Close – the famous plague street, which we'll cover later.

If you know the city there are tiny pointers to its grisly past everywhere. In Brodie's Close, for instance, there is a doorstep with a deep groove in it. It was made by soldiers sharpening their bayonets before preparing to defend the castle against the Jacobites.

Edinburgh knows the value of its dark and violent past. The *Edinburgh Dungeon* is an attraction which deals completely with nasty side of Scottish history. There are shops promoting Paganism and witchcraft. There were even plans to erect a statue to the body snatchers – though common decency prevented in the end. Even Edinburgh castle got in on the act – opening more of its dungeons and converting its military prison into a visitor centre.

Of course, the companion to a violent history is a supernatural present. You can't get closer to a horrible past than seeing someone who lost their head floating through the wall with it under his arm.

Turn on the television these days and you'd be hard pushed to find a channel that doesn't have some kind of paranormal programme. The public can't get enough of it and Edinburgh flaunts its supernatural aspects mercilessly. At present there are a dozen ghost tours operating in the city, some better than others.

So, to some extent, Edinburgh has a haunted reputation because it tries very hard to cultivate one – and it has succeeded.

But you know what they say.

There's no smoke without fire.

Chapter 10

The Underground City

Edinburgh castle was on the highest pinnacle of the Old Town ridge. The muddy road that led to it was steep and slippery and Peazle was wheezing like a donkey long before he reached the top. Though the hill was an easy climb for a hale and hearty boy, a diet of cold potatoes and gruel hadn't done much for the young pickpocket's health. Eventually the slope opened onto castle esplanade – an exposed area leading to the huge iron portcullis that fronted the massive fortress walls. Since the other three sides of the castle overlooked sheer cliff faces, the esplanade was the only real way to reach the castle - which left potential invaders horribly exposed – it was said that the approach was exactly the length an arrow could be accurately fired.

In peacetime, however, the esplanade's tremendous height made it the perfect spot for sightseeing and now the area was filled with young men trying to impress their lady friends by wearing their Sunday best and pretending to know the names of far off hills.

Peazle strolled around like the city's scruffiest tourist, secretly eyeing young men buying cups of flavoured ice for their paramours and watching where they kept their purses.

"A fool and his money are soon parted - and love makes a fool of the wisest man," the pickpocket said sagely.

Pretending to stare at the view, Peazle stretched out his hand and slowly lifted the tailcoat of the young man to his left, who was chatting animatedly to his lady. A stiff breeze blew from the Pentland Hills across the esplanade and tore at the youth's clothes, making the pickpocket's practiced manoeuvre impossible to detect. The wallet slid out of the back pocket, vanished into the boy's vest and he gave a satisfied smile – the young man was so engrossed in his beau that the Peazle could have stolen his underwear. As the boy turned to escape, the grin froze on his lips.

Two kilted soldiers stood behind him pointing their bayonets at his stomach.

Peazle had never been inside the castle before and, though he was truly impressed by the lofty battlements and smoke blackened towers, he wished at that moment he could be anywhere else on the planet. The two soldiers marched him up the winding cobbled road into the very heart of the fortifications, past endless stone barracks, cannons and cooking fires. The castle hadn't seen a battle for half a century but it was still a military garrison and kilted recruits and officers in bright tartan trews and scarlet jackets stared as the pickpocket was escorted past. The air pulsed with the smell of roasting meat and the sound of shouted orders.

"What are you going to do with me?" he asked one of the soldiers timidly.

"If it were oop ter me lad, oi'd probably joost shoot yer," he replied in a thick Irish brogue. "Boot its ter the doonguns oim taking yer."

"The dungeons!" Peazle squealed, then quickly regained his composure. Panicking wasn't going to help this situation. *"I thought they were only for prisoners of war."*

"Dat dey are," the soldier replied. *"Boot we're not at war with anyone at present and as it happens there's a coople o men down dere from the town council - so I reckon oil joost hand yis over to them."* He motioned with his bayonet towards an oak doorway set in a tower wall and the other soldier pushed Peazle through.

Behind the door a steep staircase wound into the bowels of the castle and the soldiers' tackety boots clattered on the stone as they followed Peazle round and round and down and down, past cold gaping chambers fortified with iron bars. In the darkness of some of the vaults Peazle could hear murmuring in some language he didn't understand.

"Dootch smooglers," said the talkative Irishman. *"Oi can't oondershtand a bloody werd they're saying."*

The trio eventually arrived at a long corridor lit by thick, acrid candles. A group of men, two soldiers and two civilians, were clustered round a table cluttered with paper, trying to read in the flickering light.

"Sah! The tunnel don't show up on any of the charts we have!" a soldier with a giant walrus moustache barked. The civilians gave a little jump. *"There's no telling where it might lead. Might be a few feet or..."*

"...Or it might lead right under our defences, yes sergeant." The other soldier, an officer of some sort, folded his hands behind his back. *"We simply have to find out where it goes. Can't fit any of our men in there you say?"*

"No Sah!" The civilians winced again. *"Not even Private Hemmingway - an he lost his legs at Waterloo."* The sergeant thought for a second before adding, *"and an arm."*

The officer sighed. The sergeant turned to Peazle and his guards. *"What are you doing with that boy private MacSorry?"*

"Caught him stealing sor. Wallets. Oop on the esplanade."

"That's not a military matter, private," said the officer, brusquely.

"I know sor and I tot since dere were two members of the town council here, oid bring him to dem."

The councillors, dressed in identical breeches and frock coats, looked up from the charts.

"It's not our concern soldier," one said. "Deliver him to the town guard. He'll most likely be tried by the magistrate on Monday."

The officer stroked his moustache thoughtfully before speaking. "What will happen to the boy?"

"It's a serious charge, pickpocketing, if he was caught red handed," the councillor went back to studying the charts. "He'll be deported to a penal colony in Australia, like as not."

Peazle raised his hand. "Actually I was just testing these fine soldiers' powers of observation and very alert they were too. I was going to put the money back...."

"Don't even bother lad." The officer crouched down beside Peazle and put a hand on his shoulder. "But there might be a way we could forget this whole ehm... incident."

"Oh I don't think that's possible." The councillor looked up again "Boy broke the law."

"What I'm proposing son." The officer ignored the interruption. "Is for you to redeem yourself by a bit of bravery. Like a little soldier, eh?" Peazle nodded enthusiastically, not having a clue what the officer was talking about. Encouraged, the man continued.

"We've found a tunnel in the dungeons lad, didn't even know it was there. And we need to know where it goes but it's too small for any of my men to fit in, see?" Peazle nodded again, more slowly this time - he was beginning to understand what the officer was getting at.

"So if you was to have a little explore of this tunnel and tell us where it went, the army would consider this an act of patriotism – a great civic duty. Isn't that right, gentlemen?"

Now the councillors were nodding as well. Private MacSorry gave Peazle a thumbs up sign.

"True. A boy would be forgiven a bit of thievery if he was as patriotic as that," one councillor said slyly. "Wouldn't get sent to Australia neither."

Peazle looked from one looming adult to another. They leaned towards him, moustaches bristling.

"All right," said the pickpocket wearily. "Show me the tunnel."

"Wait a moment. How will we know where he's gone?" the other official spoke.

"Drum, Sah!" screamed the sergeant and the councillors jumped again. "There's a tiny drum in the officers mess, it was made for Colonel Grouper's little boy – before he blew his head off playing with a loaded musket!"

"All right, sergeant. Fetch the drum and a firebrand for the lad." The officer leaned further towards Peazle. "We're going to make a hero of you son, rather than a villain," he whispered, not unkindly.

The firebrand sputtered badly and the narrowness of the tunnel deflected the heat back into Peazle's face - he was forced to hold the torch as far in front of him as he could and crawl using his free arm. The leather strap attached to the drum kept getting tangled in his legs and the only way he could make a noise was to stop crawling and kick at the drum's taught skin with his feet.

The councilmen and soldiers at the entrance to the tunnel waited until the erratic banging was so faint they could hardly hear it.

"Sergeant," the officer said finally. "Take some men and scour the main courtyard, see if they can pick up the noise there. Put some out on the esplanade too."

"Yes Sah!" The sergeant stood to attention, then hesitated. "Beggin your pardon Sah, but that drum the lad's dragging behind him, fills the entire tunnel. If it comes to a dead end how's he going to get back?"

"This is a military garrison." The officer gave the sergeant a withering look. *"We can't just have tunnels running who knows where. We need to know where it goes."* Then he turned and walked away.

Wriggling along the tiny passageway Peazle was soon close to exhaustion - the firebrand in front of him was burning precious oxygen, what air he could suck into his straining lungs was hot and thin, and his elbows and knees throbbed where the rough stone had torn away the skin. Worst of all, he was gripped by a rising panic that was becoming harder and harder to quell - he wanted to scream in rage and fear and thrash at the walls but he knew that this would use up even more air. Instead he forced himself to lie still until he felt a semblance of calm return. Then he began to crawl forward once more.

Finally, when the pickpocket had almost given up hope, the little passage began to widen. Soon Peazle could crawl on his hands and knees, then manage a crouching shuffle and, finally, he was able to stand. He put the torch on the ground, fastened the drum round his waist and untied the drumsticks strapped to his thigh.

On the esplanade private MacSorry sat on a low wall rolling a cigarette.

"MacSorry!" roared the sergeant. *"I know the boy's probably dead already or his extremities are being eaten by rats but that doesn't mean you can give up looking...."* He stopped suddenly and held up a large scarred hand. *"What 's that?"*

"What's what?"

"Silence you horrible little man! the sergeant screamed. *"How am I supposed to concentrate with you wittering on!"* He dropped to his knees and pressed a hairy ear to the ground.

"That's drumming, private, that's what it is. Under the ground." He looked up, moustache quivering, and beckoned to the officer. *"Sah! Over here!"*

Peazle marched along the tunnel, firebrand raised high. Occasionally he stopped and beat the drum for a few seconds, but not very often for the sound was deafening in such an enclosed space. The boy was wary of making a loud noise at the best of times for pickpockets, out of sheer habit, didn't like to attract unwanted attention - and who knew what lurked in these passageways? But, however alarming the drumming was, Peazle was far more disconcerted by the fact that the tunnel had begun to slope steeply down. Now, with every step, he marched deeper into the bowels of the earth.

Half way down the Royal Mile, the sergeant took his ear from the ground and slowly stood up. On one side of his head his hair, matted with mud, stuck out like a small explosion. The councillors and the officer looked at him expectantly.

"The drumming kept getting fainter, Sah, like the boy was getting further and further underground." The sergeant took a deep breath. "Then it stopped."

There was silence for a few seconds before the officer turned to the officials.

"That's not an escape tunnel or a secret entrance to the castle - not if it goes down that far." He turned to the sergeant. "Order the men back to the dungeons and have them seal the passage up."

"Ehm. Begging pardon, Sah." The sergeant looked flustered, for he was not used to questioning his superiors. "Just because the drum stopped doesn't mean the boy is dead."

"No indeed, sergeant." The officer tapped an ivory-topped cane angrily against his leg. "But my priority is the defense of the castle, not the fate of some thief." He quickly turned his back, indicating that their brief conversation was over.

"Yes Sah." The sergeant motioned to MacSorry and his companions to follow and marched purposefully back up the High Street. He had seen children die before – the drummer boy of his own regiment

had been swept away in a French cannon blast at the battle of Aurer-stadt. He didn't approve, of course, but orders were orders.

(Excerpt from *Secret City* by Jan-Andrew Henderson, courtesy of Oxford University Press)

It is said that, on quiet nights, the sound of faint drumming can still be heard coming from under the Royal Mile – the ghost of the unfortunate drummer boy. Either that or it's the band practice rooms that were once round the corner in Niddry Street.

The little drummer is one of Edinburgh's most famous ghost stories – even Robert Louis Stevenson wrote about it. And it has undergone several transformations - in some versions it is a bagpipe player who is sent to his doom in the darkness. Now that I can certainly understand.

The drummer boy story is part of the lore of Edinburgh's 'Underground City'. The Underground City is the perfect place to ferment ghostly mythology for it is legendary itself.

What is it? Where is it? Why does this city have one when no others do?

The answer is typical of Edinburgh. There is an Underground City but it isn't a city and it isn't underground. It's actually a bunch of disparate elements that go up to make this conception of a town below the ground. And how it came about is a fascinating story.

Edinburgh's strange geography is fundamental to the Underground City's creation. The Old Town is built on what is called a Crag and Tail. The castle is perched on a crag of dolomite rock and a high tail of soft sandstone – with the Royal Mile on top – slopes away from it. To appreciate just how high this Old Town ridge is, look at it from Princes Street, which towers above the rest of the city.

Because the tail was made of softer material stone it could be dug into. And because it was so high up it could be excavated from the side. The horrendous overcrowding in Edinburgh meant that people would live wherever a space could be found, even if that space was below the ground. So a warren of chambers and tunnels were carved into the Old Town ridge and occupied by the poorest sections of the community.

It is hard to imagine the horrific conditions that underground dwellers suffered. In winter Edinburgh is wet freezing and windy. Within the bare stone walls of these dank and frosty cellars conditions must have been arctic. Lighting fires warmed the inhabitants but filled the vaults with acrid smoke and represented a huge safety hazard – fires were frequent and could bury a cellar's occupants under a mountain of molten timber.

In summer the chambers would have been suffocating, the air thick with flies and raw sewage seeping in from the streets above. Yet people put up with it.

There was simply no place else to go.

It wasn't until the end of the 18th century that the city expanded and, again, Edinburgh's geography was instrumental in adding to Underground City lore.

The Old Town is ringed by a number of hills and giant bridges were built to link the original ridge to these surrounding inclines. Five main bridges were constructed between 1765 and 1833 - North Bridge, South Bridge, George IV Bridge, Regent's Bridge and King's Bridge.

These viaducts were not simply built and left, but were blended into existing streets. The gaps they spanned were developed and built up with buildings being constructed above and on either side, until the mighty structures were totally concealed.

The bridges themselves are engineering marvels. The South Bridge for instance is over 1,000 feet long and is, to all intents and purposes, invisible. One 30 foot high-arch can be seen - spanning the Cowgate at the foot of Niddry Street. Another 19 giant arches are completely out of sight.

Experimenting with new technology, city engineers filled the undersides of each bridge with vaults and chambers, which quickly became inhabited as poverty stricken Highland and Irish immigrants poured into Edinburgh. A second 'Underground City' had suddenly been created, and it wasn't even underground – it just looked like it was.

Eventually, social reforms meant these hidden sections of the Old Town were emptied of their miserable human occupancy and the vaults and cellars were converted into storage spaces or sealed off.

The most remarkable thing about the Underground City was how quickly it passed into legend. What is out of sight can easily be put out of mind, and the stories of these myriad occupied vaults soon began to get mixed up with other Edinburgh tales – elements that had little to do with buried Old Town dwellings. The fabled castle tunnel became part of the story – as did other rumoured escape passages from the fortress. Abandoned 19th century rail tunnels running under the New Town, Calton Hill and Arthur's Seat became part of the myth. So did Gilmerton Cove - an underground meeting place carved out of solid rock - perhaps used by smugglers or Covenanters in hiding. On the Royal Mile are Mary Kings Close – a partially buried street and Marlin's Wynd, Edinburgh's oldest cobbled road, covered over by the Tron Church in the 17th century.

Since these things couldn't be seen any more, the legend of the Underground City expanded unchecked. A few decades after the occupants had moved out of the original underground chambers, all conception of where they actually lived had become fuzzy. Some thought that there was a hidden metropolis under their feet, complete with shops and houses. Others swore that was nothing down there at all.

As the details faded from living memory, the bones of this already mutated legend began to be fleshed out by generations of weird and wonderful myths, including the tale of the drummer boy. In a previous book - *The Town Below The Ground* – I have already covered the most famous ones.

Until recently the situation remained unchanged. Occasionally a staff member of some Royal Mile shop would descend into a cellar, move a few boxes, and find a fireplace or the outline a door or window leading absolutely nowhere. But the rest of the Underground City remained, literally, in the dark

It was only at the end of the 20th century that the Underground City was 'discovered' again. The floor of the Tron Church is intermittently removed, so Marlin's Wynd can be displayed, after being forgotten for almost 4 centuries.

Gilmerton Cove now takes visitors, Mary King's Close is open to the public and walking tour companies like City of the Dead enter the South Bridge vaults. With their usual respect for history, city developers are talking of turning the Scotland Street Rail Tunnel into an underground car park.

Dark and hidden places like Mary Kings Close and the South Bridge Vaults practically beg to have supernatural stories attached to them. What's interesting is that these tales don't involve ghosts nobody has seen for centuries.

These locations appear to be haunted today.

And so we come to the ultimate test of Edinburgh's supernatural reputation. We can't verify paranormal phenomenon from past ages but supernatural occurrences are *still* being reported regularly. I have met people from bin men to barristers who all claim to have had a spooky experience in this city.

So, let's look at the ghosts of the present.

Chapter 11

Modern Hauntings

Edinburgh's Ghosts are not all ancient. Things continue to happen in places in and around the town that cannot be explained.

Lily Seafield: *Scottish Ghosts*

Marion Duffy stood on the left hand side of the vault. The tour guide had switched off her flashlight for effect, and that effect was certainly frightening. The blackness was so oppressive that Marion couldn't see the others in the group, their presence only indicated by nervous giggling and heavy breathing a couple of feet away. She felt her six year old daughter, Claire, search for her hand and grasp it.

The atmosphere gave her a pleasant thrill of apprehension, but she was worried about the little girl. Her daughter had been determined to see the South Bridge vaults and had confidently assured her mother she would be 'perfectly not afraid'. But Marion wondered if the darkness and the undeniable tension were a bit too much.

"Don't worry Claire," she whispered to the invisible form. "It's all just for show."

In reply the tiny hand gave hers a squeeze. Marion gasped

The grip was like iron. And it got tighter and tighter until bands of pain shot up the woman's arm.

113

Too confused even to cry out, Marion struggled to pull back from the vice like clasp. She lashed out with her foot, her agony overcoming any doubts she might have about hurting her daughter.

No little girl was doing this.

Her leg sliced through empty air. Marion lost her balance and staggered backwards, crashing heavily into the woman behind her.

"Something's attacking me!" the terrified female screamed, trying to push Marion's head away. "My God, It's got a hairy face!"

Within seconds the whole vault was yelling and crashing into each other. The guide, startled, switched the flashlight back on.

Marion Duffy looked down at her hand, but the pain had gone and there was nobody holding it. She spun around in dread, trying to spot her little girl. Complete strangers, clutching each other in terror, parted with sheepish grins and she finally glimpsed her daughter through a forest of trembling knees.

Claire was standing alone, on the other side of the vault, fifteen feet from the main party.

When questioned later the girl told witnesses that she had reached out for her mother when the light went out. Someone had led the girl to the farthest corner of the vault. Claire had been too afraid to resist, though she knew that the hand holding her own did not belong to her mother.

"How did you know that?" she was asked.

"Because it had claws" the little girl replied.

At the end of the book – in the haunted location section - I have listed all the major ghosts in Edinburgh that I could find. It's a pretty impressive collection but most of the sightings took place years ago, which makes them impossible to authenticate. There are already number of books covering 'Haunted Scotland' or 'Ghostly Edinburgh' - but most contain the same information - the white lady of this or that castle has been seen frequently since her death in 16-whatever.

Who *are* the witnesses that have reported this elusive apparition? And how sober were they? I'm not saying these frequent sightings never happened but some actual evidence would be nice.

Could you imagine a book on the solar system reporting multiple sightings of a tenth planet named Urpelvis, but not giving the name or dates of who discovered it? That wouldn't wash.

Then again investigating the paranormal isn't exactly a respected scientific pursuit and I can understand how witnesses to headless green Bogle of Loch Snechie might be a bit embarrassed to give their names.

This makes my job difficult. I've had to rely on others giving me accounts of supernatural sightings that *they* collected. I can't prove how accurate they are. The sheer number of people who have claimed to have had paranormal experiences in Edinburgh is impressive in itself - but it means I could only contact a tiny fraction of them. And the fact that this is a tourist town doesn't help, as a huge percentage of modern sightings are by visitors from Outer Mongolia.

The witnesses I actually talked to seemed genuine, but how do I know for sure? A sceptic will just say that they are mistaken, or lying, or crazy. Or all three. I've been showed strange images caught on camera, but they can be explained as faulty film or tricks of the light. One of them was definitely a finger.

Even if you notice an interesting supernatural anomaly, there's always an alternative explanation. For instance, a high proportion of the ghosts reported throughout Edinburgh's history are female. Nothing too odd about that until you remember what Edinburgh's history was like. Women rarely held positions of power, rarely had a voice – were second class citizens in every way. Why so many female ghosts then? Is it true that death is, indeed, the great leveller? You can't exactly tell a female spectre to stay out of sight while the male ones nip out for a spot of haunting.

On the other hand it may be that female ghosts were reported by other women - not because they actually saw one but because, in a male donated society, it was a small attempt to even the odds. To make men think that women they treated badly might come back in death and haunt them, since they had little recourse to justice in life.

All this is academic, and the argument about whether ghosts actually exist won't be solved by this book or any other in the near future. All I can do is find out as much information as I can about Edinburgh's most 'haunted' places – and the reader can draw their own conclusions as to whether there really is something supernatural going on.

Judging by reputation, there seems to be three main areas in Edinburgh where phantoms still crop up regularly. Mary King's Close, the South Bridge and The Covenanters Prison in Greyfriars Graveyard. Between them they have racked up more supernatural sightings than the rest of Scotland put together. Add these modern paranormal occurrences to the legacy of supernatural stories that time has put beyond reach and it goes a long, long way to vindicating Edinburgh's haunted reputation.

Mary King's Close has the historical pedigree to be a genuinely supernatural site, with a story as eerie as it is famous. The close was named after Mary King, daughter of a merchant named Alexander King and its paranormal history started with the great plague of 1645.

When the first victims in the close began to show symptoms of the disease, the city elders panicked. They locked the gates at either end of the close and refused to let residents out. Instead they pushed food and water under the gates and left the inhabitants to their horrible fate. Two months later they sauntered back in, chopped up the corpses – stiff with rigor mortis – and buried the remains in the Meadows.

Naturally, people weren't keen to live there anymore and the close remained locked up for years. It was rumoured that opening the long locked gates would release the plague and, besides, everyone knew the spirits of those who had died were still inside. As Robert Louis Stevenson so eloquently put it.

And the most bogeyish part of the story is about such houses. Two generations back they still stood dark and empty; people avoided them as they passed by; the boldest schoolboy only shouted through the keyhole and made off; for within, it was supposed, the plague lay ambushed like a basilisk, ready to flow forth and spread blain and pustule through the city.

Edinburgh folklore tells of two ministers who dared to venture into Mary Kings and confront its spectral occupants. Encountering severed limbs floating in the air, they decided a hasty exit was preferable to an exorcism and left the scene.

Then in 1685 Gorge Sinclair, professor of Moral Philosophy at Glasgow University, immortalised the close in *Satan's Invisible World Discovered*. His story concerned a gentleman named Thomas Coltheart, who moved into the close along with his wife and maid.

The maid didn't last long. She threatened to quit while they were still moving in the furniture and, true to her word, left the next day. But Thomas Coltheart wasn't going to let some paltry ghost story chase him out of a better property that the one he had left.

The next day Mrs Coltheart fainted after spotting a little head floating near the door - how she phrased *that* to her husband I'd love to know. Quite naturally, he thought she was delusional but, after she had gone to bed, Thomas Coltheart also sighted the apparition. He immediately went upstairs and assured his wife that she was right after all – there was a little head in the living room! The wife promptly fainted again. With a lack of concern that would do any chauvinist proud, he bundled her into bed, got in as well – then revived her and suggested a bout of praying.

It didn't do much good. Before long the head was joined by a young child and a naked arm which tried to shake hands with Mr Coltheart. A dog, cat and several small, unnamed creatures appeared and began to dance around the room. Whether it was in formation or they all had their individual styles is not recorded.

Then they vanished

Since hallucinogenic drugs hadn't been invented yet, Mr Coltheart and his wife were forced to admit the house was haunted. Astonishingly, they didn't leave and that seemed to seal their fate. Mr Coltheart died a few weeks later, probably of insomnia.

That did it for Mary Kings Close. Its property value plummeted and the council, in desperation, offered low rents for anyone who would live there. One or two tried, only to encounter more flying body parts. The close was finally abandoned and, in 1750, fire destroyed the south stories.

Five years later the council built the Royal Exchange (now the City Chambers) on top of the ruins – covering up Pearson's Close, Alan's Close, Stewarts Close and Craig's Close in the process – which gives you some idea of just how narrow these thoroughfares were.

The City Council had hoped that traders in Parliament Square, across the road, would move to this fine new site. But underneath the fine new site were the remains of Mary Kings Close – the Wynd from Hell – and the traders stayed exactly where they were. Eventually the north part of Mary Kings Close was also blocked off and the street passed into legend as part of Edinburgh's mysterious Underground City. It is only in the last few years that the public has had limited access to the forgotten road.

That's the famous story, but how correct is it?

Not even close. Excuse the pun.

In 2003 Mary Kings was taken over by a company called the Continuum Group, who proposed opening it properly to the public. They began exhaustive research into the history of the close and came up with a rather different story from the celebrated one.

According to their research, there is no evidence of Mary King being related to Alexander King. There is no evidence of a devastating fire in 1750. Most astonishingly, there is no evidence that plague victims were locked inside and left to die. Instead, Edinburgh Council appointed doctors to the sufferers, gave them bread and ale and quarantined them at Sciennes or Boroughmuir.

As for the close being deserted in the 18th century then completely closed over? The last inhabitant was a saw maker named Andrew Chesney who finally left in 1901.

If the famous 'facts' about Mary Kings close have turned out to be wrong then what about the hauntings? Even hardened believers might want to show a bit of scepticism at dancing cats and dogs – but has anything been reported in recent times?

They certainly have. In 1992 a number of psychics visiting the street claimed to feel a 'cold spot' in the corner of one room. Not long after a film crew came to make a documentary featuring the close and brought with them a Japanese psychic named Aiko Gibo. Gibo claimed to see an apparition in the same corner. She described this 'spirit' as a young girl about ten years old, whose name was Annie. She was wearing a dirty white dress and boots (the ghost, not the Japanese woman), wanted to know why her mother had left her and where her favourite doll was. Gobo had a modern doll brought to the room and the apparition seemed greatly consoled.

Not long after a group of servicemen and their wives were being shown around Mary Kings. In the room where the ghost had been first identified one woman screamed that there was a little girl in the corner whose face was covered in sores.

This scabby orphan is now famous and has more dolls than FAO Schwartz. – it has become customary for visitors to leave a little effigy for her in the haunted corner. There are Barbies, Bratz and assorted

Trolls piled up there – which is either touching or truly disturbing, depending on your sensibilities. Continuum's research has shown that a woman called Jean Mackenzie and her unnamed daughter were quarantined in a house in Craig's Close during the Plague - which has led people to speculate that the unnamed daughter is actually Annie.

The 'Real Mary King's Close', as it is called these days, is more interested in presenting visitors with the street's fascinating history than ramping up its haunted reputation. Even so, they were able to provide me with quite a diverse list of recent supernatural sightings – mostly reported by visitors to the close.

These include scratching noises coming from inside one chimney where a young sweep is said to have died. The sound of a party or crowded tavern can sometimes be heard overhead - yet there is nothing above but the City of Edinburgh Council Chambers and, believe me, there's never a lot of merriment going on there. Mysterious 'whispers' have been heard above ground in the admissions area. A 'worried man' crops up now and then, pacing backwards and forwards along the close. A woman in black has been sighted at the foot of the street and a merchant appears to hover below the 'plague room' window (there was once a staircase on the spot). A young boy pops up at the end of the close, an unpleasant dark presence has been reported next to Andrew Chesney's house and a middle aged woman with bad knees has been sighted at the top of the stairs leading into the street.

Looks like Mary Kings Close might be as haunted as it ever was.

The second area with a modern paranormal reputation is the area round the South Bridge. The bridge was begun in 1785 and opened the next year – an amazing speed for so large and complex a structure. Niddry, Marlin and Peebles Wynds were swept away to create space for its span and two 'artificial' streets - Blair Street and Hunters Square were erected against it, completely obscuring one side. Tenements were then erected in Niddry Street on the other face, making it unrecognizable as an overpass.

The inside of the bridge is filled with vaults and chambers separated by tunnels, originally to be used as cellars and storehouses for local merchants. But the ever present overcrowding meant that gradually the uses for the vaults diversified and traders set up as cobblers, drapers, wine merchants and jewellers in the caverns.

The top of the South Bridge was lined with thriving shops but the once fashionable Cowgate below had become an overcrowded slum. Worse still, the bridge builders had made a significant error in its construction – the vaults weren't waterproof. The damp seeped in, the traders moved out and the vaults were left to the slum dwellers.

The chambers might be cold, dark, dank and smelly but they were better than living on the streets. And they were out of sight of the prosperous bustling respectability passing above.

So people began living there.

Conditions for those residing inside the South Bridge were deplorable. It cellars teemed with beggars and urchins. Lighting was in the form of candles made of animal fat, which must have smelled pretty bad. Add five or six unwashed bodies and a toilet that was a bucket in the corner and you can imagine what the stench was like

According to Edinburgh lore many of the bridge dwellers were trapped inside the vaults by the great fire of 1824 and died of suffocation – causing the authorities to finally lock the chambers up. There is no evidence of this, however, for the fire spread in the opposite direction. As late as 1850, there are accounts of families living underground in this area. In 1845 George Bell M.D. - an early social reformer - published a horrific account of life in Blackfriars Wynd, next to the South Bridge.

In a vault or cave under a large tenement, reside an old man, his invalid wife, and his two daughters, one of whom has a natural child and the other of whom is paralytic. The man has an air of respectability about him, but the family has no visible means of living. There

were three beds in the vault; and on investigating the matter, (we) found that the said vault is a lodging house, and is often tenanted to repletion. This man is the type of class who live by subletting their miserable and dark abodes to as many as can be crammed into them. In another vault in the wynd we found a very fat Irishwoman, a widow, a pauper, and the mother of six children. By her own confession she occasionally takes in a lodger - in reality, however, she accommodates two or three all the year round.

In the late 19th century social reform finally emptied the bridges of its miserable human cargo. They were sealed up and all but forgotten until in the 20th century – only the ones nearest the street were put to public use. And public is the appropriate word - the vaulted chambers were intimate and atmospheric – the perfect place to have a pub. Later it was discovered that the thick stone walls made excellent sound-proofing for clubs and some chambers were even rented out as practice rooms for bands.

Not that thick stone chambers don't have drawbacks. I remember being in Millionaires Nightclub (now gone) in the 1970's. The cigarette smoke had nowhere to evaporate to and, by the end of the night, you needed an aqualung to breathe and a heavy duty flashlight to see through the fog.

Behind the clubs and pubs, however, there were vaults which looked the same as they did in the 19th century, so it was only a matter of time before someone took advantage of this wonderfully dark and creepy location.

Visitors can now view the South Bridge vaults of South Niddry Street by going on a City of the Dead ghost tour.

With ghost tour companies entering the South Bridge, it was probably inevitable it would gain a haunted reputation. But the weird stories had been around even before they began. 'Bloody' George Mackenzie – the scourge of the Covenanters and one of Edinburgh's famous ghosts - lived across the street. The area has always been famous for unexplained fires – and poltergeist activity has often been blamed. In 1824, the great fire of Edinburgh which destroyed the upper Royal Mile started in Old Assembly Close, just over the road. The Scandic Hotel in Niddry Street suffered a serious fire which destroyed the roof, a gas explosion blew up part of the Cowgate in the 1980's and another huge fire ravaged it in 2002.

Then there are the hauntings. The laundry room of the hostel in Blackfriars street (now gone) had a presence. The storerooms of the shop *What Everyone Wants* (also gone) had a mischievous spirit that used to move things around and was especially fond of earrings – though it's hard to be scared of a ghost that likes earrings.

Whistle Binkies, one of the pubs built into the bridge vaults, has two ghosts. The 'Imp' is a poltergeist like entity that moves things around, but since *What Everyone Wants* was right above it's probably just the earring pincher again. The 'Watcher' is a 17th or 18th century man who appears in the pub and usually heads into the cellars below. I have interviewed people who swear they have seen him and one even drew a picture of the ghostly gentleman.

Inside the vaults themselves several different figures have been seen by visitors, while others claim to have been poked or prodded. For the sake of easy categorization, Mercat Tours have lumped all the sightings under the name of 'Mr Boots' while City of the Dead have plumped for the more formal 'South Bridge Entity'.

I interviewed several visitors who claimed to have experiences in the South Bridge Vaults and their stories were recounted in my first book *The Town Below the Ground: Edinburgh's Legendary Underground City*.

I don't deny it's very convenient that the most haunted places in Edinburgh are linked to ghost tours. Then again, where are you going to take a ghost tour? Through a sunlit field of daffodils?

The fact is, Mary Kings Close and the South Bridge area both had ghostly reputations before the tours moved in. And the same is true of the last paranormal location we're going to explore.

Greyfriars Graveyard.

Chapter 11

City of the Dead

Greyfriars is the most haunted spot in the country's most haunted city

The Weekly News

On Saturday 12th January, I undertook a tour into Greyfriars Graveyard and it has changed my life. I am an experienced police officer who has attended numerous scenes of murder and fatal accidents, and have what I believe is a good common sense.

I noticed a young girl at the front right (of the Black Mausoleum). She seemed to be getting distressed and the assembled crowd heard her state "I must get out of here." I must admit I thought the young girl was suffering from claustrophobia and preconceived fear.

After the tour my wife Gillian and I decided to go back to our hotel room. I was glancing occasionally at 'The Ghost That Haunted Itself' (the story of the Mackenzie Poltergeist). I suddenly felt a sharp burning sensation on the right hand side of my neck. There were at least five deep scrapes.

Gillian had nodded off to sleep. Suddenly I heard what appeared to be a woman's voice crying 'Brecky' or 'Becky'.

Gillian sat up behind me and exclaimed, "What was that, did you hear that?" She said the voice had woken her up.

About two hours later, still not sleeping, I heard the horrible al-most whispered voice of a woman, who sounded as if she was shivering violently, saying "help me, help me."

I whispered the Lord's Prayer out loud, which for a non-churchgoer and general non-believer was a vain attempt at some divine assistance!

On returning home that morning I went straight to my mother's house with Gillian and told her my tale, along with handing her the book The Ghost That Haunted Itself, *which I had decided I did not want in my home.*

My mother is a remarkably practical Belfast born mother of four. Yesterday I phoned her and asked her what she thought of the book. She was examining 5 large scratches on her neck. My mother stated that, as she woke up, she felt a 'burning sensation'. On examination, she discovered the same five scratches I had received and in the same location as my own,

I am not the sort of individual who frightens easily but, hand on heart, I am very frightened now. The phenomenon in that graveyard prison is <u>very real</u>

Please do not use my real name for security reasons – I am pre-pared to talk to anyone who wishes to ask me anything. I would take a lie detector test, anything! I have photographic proof, I have witness proof and I trust that will be enough.

-Excerpts from a nine page letter by a Belfast Policeman who visit-ed Greyfriars Graveyard.

I started reading the book (The Ghost That Haunted Itself). *I start-ed to feel there was another person in the room, and I felt really cold. 'Somebody' said "NO" out loud. That was the night that I decided not to read the book anymore.*

Also I had scratches on my chest and arms and I still don't know how they got there.

- Excerpt from an email sent by Lutske Van der Ley, Holland

Over the last five years one small tomb in Greyfriars Cemetery has become famous as the lair of a malevolent paranormal entity. The tomb is known as the 'Black Mausoleum' and is located behind the high walls and locked gates of an area known as the Covenanters Prison.

The entity has been named 'The Mackenzie Poltergeist'.

I will readily admit to having a soft spot for the Mackenzie Poltergeist. I've already written a book about it – *The Ghost that Haunted Itself* (though I'm not sure I liked the policeman's reaction to my efforts). I used to live in a house in the graveyard right across from the Covenanter Prison. Not that I'm weird or anything like that – the rent was cheap. I even started City of the Dead walking tours to investigate the phenomenon.

Sounds obsessive but, honestly, it isn't. Most authors who write about a famous supernatural case (should they be crazy enough) are unfamiliar with the location, the people involved and the more intimate details of the situation. Here I was living a few feet away from a paranormal case that was attracting massive media attention. It was too good an opportunity to turn down.

Not long after the initial sightings of the Mackenzie Poltergeist, the Covenanters Prison was locked by City of Edinburgh Council. I obtained permission to set up tours that would unlock and enter the site - to see if anything unexplained happened. It also gave me access to every witness to any paranormal phenomena.

If something unexplained happened to a visitor in the Covenanters Prison, the tour guide would take their name, address and statement. We even developed a control experiment. While telling people about the entity the guides would include a false piece of information about typical supernatural occurrences. If this detail cropped up in a witness statement, we concluded that this particular onlooker was trying a little too hard and disregarded it.

In short, I had the perfect set up to study an alleged paranormal location as well as the entity it supposedly contained.

Some of my more superstitious friends think I paid a high price for that. But I'm getting ahead of myself.

Like Roslin, Greyfriars Graveyard has the reputation as a Thin Place. Like Roslin it seems to have too much influence for one small location – too grand a history for its size. And, in Greyfriars case, too grisly a history.

During the great plague of 1568, thousands of diseased corpses were flung into a huge pit there. One of the two entrances looks out across the old execution sight in the Grassmarket and the heads of condemned criminals were displayed on poles at the gate before being buried back inside. In 1581 James Douglas, Regent of Scotland, was guillotined outside the North Gate for the murder of the Mary Queen of Scots' husband, and his headless body was buried with the common crooks. The actual murder took place at a spot where the south wall now stands.

In 1637 the Scots Presbyterians signed the 'National Covenant with God' in the graveyard and embarked on their religious crusade against the south. Their initial success eventually led to the English Civil war and the execution of Charles I. It was also instrumental in establishing Presbyterianism as a religious movement – one that spread across the continent of America. In fact, the National Covenant's influence is such that, when it is pared down, it contains exactly the same words as the Preamble to the Constitution of the United States of America.

Within 50 years, however, the Covenanter movement was broken and Charles II crushed their last army at the Battle of Bothwell Brig. Twelve hundred survivors were imprisoned in the Covenanter's Prison' without proper shelter or food – making it, in effect, the world's first concentration camp.

A total of 18,000 Covenanters died for their beliefs - most put to death by the King's Advocate, 'Bloody' George Mackenzie. In 1691, Mackenzie was buried in Greyfriars - right next to the Covenanter's Prison and not far from dozens of their graves.

This gave rise to another of Edinburgh's older ghost stories, also retold by Robert Louis Stevenson. It is said that the coffin moves around under the great tomb - for 'Bloody' Mackenzie can never find rest after the atrocities he committed.

In the early 18th century the graveyard was the haunt of the Resurrection Men or Body Snatchers. They would silently scrape away the earth with wooden spades, prise open one end of the coffin and slide the body out using hooks and ropes – an anatomist would pay less for damaged goods. The corpse would be bundled away, the hole filled in and Greyfriars would be left with one more small tale of tragedy in its collection. Today you can still see 'mortislocks' - cage like devices intended to protect new bodies until they had rotted sufficiently to be useless for dissection.

In December 1879, the city authorities dumped the contents of St Giles' graveyard, several tons of remains, into Greyfriars - including, quite possibly, John Knox himself. Well, he never did go for pomp and ceremony.

In fact the number of people buried in Greyfriars well exceeded its capacity – for centuries it was the only graveyard in the most over-crowded spot in Europe.

If you go there now you find yourself standing on a steep hill over-looking the Old Town. In fact, the hill used to be valley. We will never know how many people are buried inside (there are only a few hundred headstones) – but there may well be hundreds of thousands.

Greyfriars is literally a mountain of dead people.

I'm not saying Thin Places actually exist, but Greyfriars is a per-fect candidate if they do. If there *are* sites where this world and the world of the paranormal are closest, it may not be a great idea to fill them with hundreds of thousands of bodies.

I recall telling this to an Australian girl in the cemetery. She looked across at the Covenanters Prison.

"Perhaps something has finally come through from the other side," she said.

I must admit, it was a chilling line.

The Black Mausoleum seems to differ from Edinburgh's other haunted locations for two reasons. One is the frequency of the poltergeist sightings. The other is the severity of the incidents. The period between the first recorded sightings in 1999 and the present, have seen hundreds of documented 'attacks' in the Black Mausoleum and Covenanters Prison. Of these attacks, an astonishing 150 have caused the witness to collapse.

Over the years there have been multiple reports of hot spots, cold spots and cuts, bruises and burns on witnesses' bodies – often under their clothes. Photographs have been taken of these marks as well as many pictures of an unidentified shape in the tomb. There have been sightings of a white figure, unexplained smells, and auditory anomalies - including knocking noises under the ground and inside the tomb itself. Dead animals are found, unmarked, in front of the Black Mausoleum. People have complained that an unseen entity has pulled their hair, grabbed their legs and arms and hit, burned or bit them. One or two have even claimed to be possessed. The area has been exorcised twice – both times unsuccessfully.

Poltergeist activity has been reported in four different houses around the graveyard and a large fire broke out in the residences behind George Mackenzie's tomb in 2002.

Then in October 2003 a fire swept through my house overlooking the graveyard. It destroyed five years worth of letters, photographs, records and statements concerning the Mackenzie Poltergeist as well as every possession I had in the world. None of the surrounding properties were damaged and an official cause for the fire has not been established.

So I started again. I'll not be put off by something that hangs around in a tomb. Mind you, I live in Australia now.

Eventually the sheer number of sightings became so large that City of the Dead stopped collecting eyewitness reports on the tours themselves. But we still get dozens of emails from people reporting what happened to them, including numerous chilling photographs of the injuries inflicted on the customers.

I don't know what the Mackenzie Poltergeist really is. I don't know if it's a supernatural entity, a pheromone cloud, a demon or a set of psychosomatic and hysterical reactions. All have been suggested. But I know it has become the best documented supernatural case of all time and probably the most conclusive.

Let me put it this way – if the Mackenzie Poltergeist isn't a genuine supernatural entity then I don't think there's any such thing. Not anywhere in the world.

If it is real, it seems feasible that many of Edinburgh's other ghosts are real too. Going by the sheer number of modern sightings, its haunted reputation is pretty secure anyway. Not that this city needs to be haunted to keep its eerie reputation, we've already seen that.

And if, one day, we prove without a shadow of a doubt that ghosts don't exist? If we know for certain that Edinburgh's haunted reputation is based on a chimera?

I'm sure the city will get over it.

It's been through a lot worse.

Chapter 12

Haunted Locations

May the forces of evil become confused on the way to your house

George Carlin

The following sections give the locations of Edinburgh's darkest events and its most famous haunted sites. Where the original buildings have been destroyed the estimated location is given. Unfortunately, the very nature of ghost stories make them as elusive as their subjects. The Green Lady of this or that mansion may be famous, but sometimes it's difficult tell if her fame is due to multiple sightings or being seen once by some drunken laird in the 17th century who told the story repeatedly to anyone who would listen.

For whatever reason, however, all the following are established parts of Edinburgh's supernatural lore.

The Old Town

The Old Town is stuffed full of supernatural locations. Since this small part of the modern city *was* Edinburgh for most of its history, there are far more horrific stories (and ghosts) recorded here than anywhere else. It also has a few supernatural tales not tied down to any one location – such as a fiery death coach which appears before a disaster and gallops down the street pulled by headless horses.

Won't be hailing that one, then.

133

Edinburgh Castle.

The castle is haunted by several apparitions. This is hardly surprising given its history of conflict and the fact that there has been some sort of fortification on castle rock since prehistory.

John Graham of Claverhouse is said to haunt the ramparts. He was known as 'Bloody Clavers' because of his ruthless persecution of Covenanters in the 17th century – along with his accomplice 'Bloody' George Mackenzie.

When James II of Scotland was deposed, Claverhouse made a momentous about-turn and raised a Catholic highland army to fight for his king. He was killed leading a magnificent highland charge at the battle of Killiekrankie in 1689 and, because of this, is better known in Scots lore as 'Bonny' Dundee. He was first seen in the castle on the night of his death by Lord Balcarres, who was in charge of the castle's Jacobite prisoners, and has appeared periodically from then on.

That same year the Duke of Gordon, governor of the Castle, stabbed his steward for bringing news of his family's death. The unfortunate man now wanders the walls. Some employees are just impossible to get rid of.

The castle, it seems, is afflicted by all sorts of military themed spooks. Phantom drumming was first heard in 1650 and the castle was taken by Oliver Cromwell's forces soon after – leading to the idea that this was a portent for disaster. In later sightings the drummer is sometimes invisible, sometimes headless and was last reported in the 1960s. The ramparts also boast ghostly bagpiping and the invisible marching of massed men. The dungeons are said to be plagued by the ghosts of prisoners held during the Napoleonic Wars and blue orbs have been captured on film.

The castle is also haunted by Janet Douglas, Lady Glamis. A member of the Douglas family, long distrusted by the Stuart kings, she was accused of witchcraft on a trumped up charge and burned at the stake in 1537 in front of her husband and son. A busy ghost, she also finds time to haunt Glamis Castle in Angus.

The Castle Esplanade.

This was the site where witches were burned, including poor old Janet Douglas. It is estimated that around 300 witches and heretics were strangled then burned on Castlehill. Today a small well at the end of the esplanade is the only monument to those unfortunate souls.

St John's Tollbooth Church, Castlehill, Royal Mile.

A whipping site. The Witchery Tours leave next to the church

Brodie's Close.

The home of William 'Deacon' Brodie. Now the site of *Brodie's Café*. Across the street is *Deacon Brodie's Bar*.

Lawnmarket.

Site of Edinburgh's last public hanging in 1864. There is a legend of a Marie Celeste style house here. In the 18th century one of the flats was suddenly abandoned in panic, right in the middle of a dinner party. The exit was so hasty that half eaten food was left on the table, though those who fled did lock the door behind them – a door that was never reopened. I must admit this bit of the legend puzzles me. If the door was never unlocked again, how do we know what was left on the table?

By the 19th century the story had passed into lore with Robert Chambers writing 'No one knows to whom the house belongs; no one ever inquires after it, no one living ever saw the inside of it, it is a condemned house." Unfortunately it really was condemned and no longer exists.

Heart of Midlothian, Royal Mile.

Heart shaped stones in the ground mark the site of Edinburgh's notorious Tolbooth Prison. It was also a place of executions (including the Marquises of Montrose and Argyll, Deacon Brodie and William Burke)

St Giles' Cathedral, Royal Mile.

Covenanters were imprisoned here in *Haddo's Hole*. The 'Maiden' (Scotland's version of the guillotine) was kept here.

City of the Dead Tours leave from this site.

City Chambers, Royal Mile.

Underneath are the remains of *Mary King's Close,* the famous haunted street.

Mercat Cross, Royal Mile.

Public whippings and beheadings took place here. This was the site where, in 1513, a ghostly herald appeared to Richard Lawson and predicted the disastrous battle of Flodden. Auld Nick read out a list of all those who were going to die on the battle field, including James IV and Lawson himself – at which point the unfortunate man sank to his knees and prayed for salvation.

Some say it was a hoax by Queen Margaret to try and prevent her husband going to war. If so, it failed. The king went and so did Lawson, probably bedecked with every lucky charm he could find. He was one of the few Scots to survive the massacre. James IV perished - as did fifteen earls, seventy lords and 10,000 men. The present Mercat Cross only dates from 1885. The original was further down the street.

Fishmarket Close, Royal Mile.

John Scott (Edinburgh's last hangman) lived here – he was murdered in 1856.

This was also the workplace of 'Half Hangit' Maggie Dixon. In 1724 she got pregnant and abandoned her new born baby. Tried under the concealment of Pregnancy act of 1690 (yes there was such a thing) she was found guilty, sentenced to death and hanged. Surprisingly, she sat up in the back of the cart on the way to the cemetery. This caused a legal furore in the city but it was decided that, since she had already been pronounced dead, they couldn't hang her again. She lived for a further 30 years and even opened her own pub. Today there is a bar in the Grassmarket called *Maggie Dixon's* but it is not in the same location as the original.

Bells Wynd, Royal Mile

In 1780 a tenant in one of the tenements, George Gourlay, repeatedly approached his landlord with what he thought was a reasonable request. His family was growing and he wished to rent the empty flat below his. His landlord, Patrick Guthrie always said no, but refused to give a reason for the rebuttal. In frustration Gourlay broke into the flat and found a ghostly female figure standing in the middle of the room. He was so frightened that he reported what he had done to the procurator fiscal. An investigation discovered the corpse of Patrick Guthrie's wife in the empty flat. He had killed her when he found out she'd been having an affair.

Old Assembly Close, Royal Mile.

This is where the great fire of 1824 started, burning for three days and destroying most of the upper Royal Mile. The scorch marks can still be seen on the doorway of the Tron Church across the street.

The Tron Church, Royal Mile.

Criminals had their ears nailed to a wooden weigh beam here.

The Scotsman Hotel, North Bridge.

Formerly the Scotsman Newspaper Office, which seemed to have a whole plethora of ghosts. In 1990 security guard ran into an employee who he knew to be dead. In 1994 a page make up artist, working in the basement, came across a door he had never seen before. Upon entering he stumbled upon a phantom printer sporting old fashioned clothes and beard and carrying antiquated printing plates. The building was also haunted by a blonde woman in a blonde dress who would vanish any time a member of staff came over to ask what she wanted. Apparently there is also a phantom forger.

Then again, you can't believe everything you read in the press.

The South Bridge.

Vaults inside the bridge are said to be haunted by a faceless man and a mischievous poltergeist.

Radisson Blu (Formerly Scandic Crown) Hotel, Niddry Street.

Stands on the site of Strichen's Close – home of 'Bloody' George Mackenzie. This entire area has been plagued by fires, not only the great fire of 1824, but numerous others. The hotel itself has suffered extensive damage in 1987 and a massive fire in 2002 destroyed the bottom of the street.

Whistle Binkie's Bar, Niddry Street.

This bar, made out of 19th century converted bridge vaults, is haunted by a long haired gentleman in 17th century attire. He is called the Watcher but no one has ever seen his face. This bar and the storerooms of South Bridge shops are also home to an entity known as the Imp. This mischievous creature stops clocks, slams doors and moves objects. Sightings began in the early 90's and continue to this day.

Former Royal Mile Backpackers Hostel, Blackfriars Street.

Reputed to have a haunted laundry room. Sightings began in the 1980's and continue to this day.

St Mary's Street.

Haunted by the victim of an apparently motiveless murder. A young woman was killed here in 1916 by an assailant who leapt out of a doorway, stabbed her and ran off, without robbing her or molesting her in any other way. She is still seen occasionally, her clothes splattered with blood, an understandably astonished expression on her face.

The Museum of Childhood, Royal Mile.
The area behind this building is said to ring with the voices of crying children late at night. During the plague years an outbreak occurred in a nearby nursery, which was sealed up with the children and mothers inside.

Bailie Fyfe's Close, Royal Mile.
Site of the *Heave Awa' disaster* in 1861 – when a tenement collapsed burying 135 people. Famously, as rescuers pulled at the rubble, they heard a young voice crying far under the debris. "Heave awa' lads, I'm no' dead yet!" A bust of the plucky survivor can still be seen over the close entrance.

Chessels Court, Royal Mile.
Site of Deacon Brodie's last botched robbery at the Edinburgh Excise Office. In the late 19th century, the tenements that stand there were haunted by a woman wearing a black silk veil – identified as an occupant who had recently hanged herself.

Netherbow Port, Royal Mile.
One of the gates to the city was here, and it was the site of public executions. Body parts of the deceased were displayed on top of the port as a warning to other wrongdoers. Brass cobbles mark the location of the gate.

The Netherbow is the site of the *World's End Pub*. Two teenagers drinking there in 1977 were later found murdered in East Lothian.

The Canongate, Royal Mile.

Haunted by a burning woman. She was the daughter of an influential family in the 18th century but had the misfortune to fall pregnant by a servant. A minister was called to deliver last Rites to the girl, which he objected to, since she looked perfectly healthy. He was given money and threatened to keep his mouth shut. Later that day the girl was killed when an 'accidental' fire burned the house down. The house was rebuilt but caught fire again many years later. In the heart of the conflagration the girl appeared, screaming "Once burnt, twice burnt, the third time I'll scare you all!" The third fire has, so far, not occurred.

Queensbury House, Canongate.

Haunted by a kitchen boy who was roasted and eaten by James Douglas, the lunatic Earl of Drumlanrig - son of the Duke of Queensbury. At the time the Duke was arranging the union of Scottish and English parliaments in 1707 – an act so loathed by the Edinburgh people that they rioted in the streets and cursed his house. Ironically Queensbury House is now incorporated into the long delayed and grossly over budget Scottish Parliament building.

So, no change there then.

Holyrood Palace.

This has an excellent class of ghost – being haunted by Mary Queen of Scots, her husband Lord Darnley and her secretary David Rizzo – all of whom came to violent ends. Lowering the tone is the naked ghost of Bald Agnes, who was stripped and tortured in 1592 after being accused of witchcraft.

The Cowgate.

Site of the *Cleansing of the Causeway* in 1524 – Scotland's largest street fight in which hundreds of participants were killed. The area is haunted by an unnamed man with rope burns round his neck.

West Bow (Victoria Street).

Anderson's Close, demolished in 1827, was the home of Major Thomas Weir (The Wizard of the West Bow). It was also 'Stinking Close' and after repeated sightings of spectres came to be known as 'Haunted Close'.

The West Bow is also haunted by a phantom coach and the ghost of a sailor named Angus Roy. Crippled on a voyage in 1820, he settled in this area and spent the next 20 years there until his death. He longed for the sea and was tormented by local children who mimicked his severe limp. He is still seen occasionally, dragging his injured leg behind him. It's a shame he picked such a steep street to haunt.

Grassmarket.

This was the site where Covenanters were executed and a circular monument set into the ground commemorates these tragic events. It was also the place of public hangings and the cleverly named *Last Drop* pub is behind the spot. The *White Hart Inn*, where the mass murderers William Burke and William Hare reputedly picked up victims in the 1820's still stands. The area is haunted by a woman with a burned face and the phantom coach that gallops down the West Bow sometimes carries on through the Grassmarket.

Market Street.

Location of the *Edinburgh Dungeon*

High Riggs, West Port.

This was the site of *Tanner's Close*, demolished in 1902. In the close was the lodging house where Burke and Hare killed their victims, then sold their bodies to Edinburgh University Anatomy Department

George IV Bridge.

Number 21 is The *Elephant House* where *Harry Potter and the Philosophers Stone* was written

Bridge vaults under the National Library of Scotland are haunted by an unidentified highland chief. When he was spotted by librarian Elizabeth Clarke, in 1973, she noticed that his hands were manacled. The bridge vaults were used in the 19th century to imprison debtors.

Greyfriars Graveyard.

Burial place of Sir George Mackenzie. The site of the *Covenanter's Prison* – the world's first concentration camp. Inside is the Black Mausoleum, lair of the Mackenzie Poltergeist.

Bedlam Theatre, Forest Road.

Near the site of a former asylum. Haunted by a shadowy figure that flits through the theatre.

(Almost every theatre in Edinburgh, even those which have been demolished, has some sort of ghost story attached. This, however, is true of theatres in any city. It's just one of those things).

Potterrow.

Agnes Finney lived in a house here, now demolished. She was burned as a witch in 1644

The New Town

The New Town wasn't built until the 18th century and consequently has less ghostly lore. Populated by well-to-do Georgians and then Victorians, the ghosts here generally have a more genteel and well mannered disposition, as befitted the times.

George Street.

Haunted by Jane Vernelt in the early 20th century. She lost her shop here after bad financial advice from friends and died shortly after. She was seen several times in broad daylight, heading towards the now non-existent property.

House number 81 was where the playboy Eugene Chantrelle poisoned his wife in 1877. He was hanged for the offence.

At number 60 a plaque commemorates the fact that the poet Shelley honeymooned here with his first wife in 1811 – at the height of the bodysnatching period. Soon after she committed suicide and Shelly married the author of *Frankenstein*.

Charlotte Square.

This square has seen a number of recorded phantoms including a ghost coach, a beggar, a woman and a monk. The sound of ghostly piano playing can also be heard. The possibility that someone in one of the buildings is actually playing the piano has, apparently, never been considered.

The Learmonth Hotel, Queensferry Street.

Plagued by a whistling poltergeist that opens and closes doors.

15 Learmonth Gardens.

Edinburgh even has its own Mummy's Curse! In the 1930's the house belonged to Alexander Hay Seaton, 10th Baronet of Abercorn. On a trip to Egypt in 1936 his wife Zelda secretly picked up a bone from a tomb that was being excavated. On their return, the bone was displayed in a glass case in the dining room.

From that moment the house was plagued by accidents, broken furniture, unexplained noises and flying objects – all carefully recorded by Seaton. There were even a few appearances by a spectral figure that looked like an ancient Egyptian priest. Seaton kept a careful account of the strange happenings and came to firmly believe that the artefact was cursed. The bone was finally exorcised and then destroyed – but it did not help the unfortunate Baronet, who later wrote

"The curse did not end with the destruction of the bone. From 1936 onwards trouble always seemed to beset me."

St John's Churchyard and West End of Princes Street.

A crying woman has been reported throughout the 20th century, spectral in appearance. Grieving for her murdered husband – struck down in the area - she stumbled in front of a horse and carriage on the same spot and was also killed.

No 5 Rothesay Place.

In 1958 the Van Horne family purchased some second hand furniture that had belonging to a recently deceased sailor. Soon after strange tapping sounds began, ornaments placed on the furniture moved around, the smell of tobacco smoke permeated the dwelling and a bright ball of light was occasionally spotted. Eventually a tiny foot-high figure began to make appearances, dressed in a brown jacket and red trousers. The Van Hornes, without apparent concern for their own safety, gave him the ignominious nickname of Gnomey. The occurrences came to a halt in 1960.

In the relatively short time since, the legend has already developed variations – some accounts say the ghost has the equally embarrassing moniker of Merry Jack Tar and it haunts the flat because of an old piece of wood brought back from a seaside cottage in the north of Scotland.

Hope Street.

Haunted by a woman called Moira Blair – though apparently only in the evenings. She sometimes gets blamed for the crying coming from St John's churchyard.

Heriot Row.

Reports of hauntings here began in 1981. The new occupants, who had just moved in, noticed that the shutters on the windows of Georgian house kept opening even though nobody was near them. Exploring the house, they came across a secret compartment and, when they opened it, eerie sounds echoed through the building before dying away. You think the surveyor might have mentioned that.

Jamaica Street.

Haunted in the late 18th/early 19th century by a man with a bright red hat. The landlord of one of the houses there actually took his tenant James Campbell to court over the matter. He claimed that the sartorially challenged ghost had been made up by Campbell in order to keep the rent low. Despite the fact that Campbell produced witnesses to back up his story, he was fined £5 and told not to mention the ghost again.

Royal Circus.

A spectral woman kept appearing and disappearing in the buildings being renovated here - upsetting workmen so much that they called in a medium to investigate. After the medium 'made contact' the young woman was never seen again.

Buckingham Terrace.

Haunted by the ghost of an old sailor. The Gordon family, who lived in a flat there in the 19th century, were constantly disturbed by banging noises. A menacing but indistinct figure was sometimes seen in the furniture store above their house, often next to an antique grandfather clock. This frayed the family's nerves so much that they eventually moved out.

It was later discovered that the house had belonged to an alcoholic sailor. It was alleged that he had been awakened by a crying child one night. In a fit of rage, he had shaken her to death and tried to hide her body in the clock casing. He was arrested and sent to a lunatic asylum, where he later committed suicide.

No 12 Anne Street.

Haunted by a small man dressed in black called Mr Swan. He was a former resident in the 19th century but died overseas. He popped up at his old house over the years and was eventually exorcised, though all he did was hang around smiling.

The exorcism seemed to work until the house was sold in 1936, and then Mr Swan began to appear again. Perhaps he liked the new occupants better for the children there often claimed that he would come and say goodnight to them when they went to bed. Cause *that's* not creepy.

Former Post Office building, Waterloo Place.

Built on the site of the *Theatre Royal*, which reputedly held phantom performances after the official show had finished. It was demolished in 1866.

Regent Terrace.

In 1979 one of the flats here was plagued by poltergeist activity. Crying and breathing noises came from empty rooms. Small valuables would vanish for days on end and something small and unseen would jump on beds when the occupants were in them. The people who lived there were eventually driven out.

No 56 India Street.

Haunted by a frequently seen entity floating in the hall, but so shadowy it can't be identified as a man or woman. It only turns up whenever there are dinner parties or social occasions in the building, which makes it a typical New Town resident.

The 'Burbs

The rest of Edinburgh varies in age. Some districts are new. Others were outlying villages swallowed by the capital's expansion. The burgh of Leith, for instance, is as old as the Old Town but was only incorporated into the city in 1920. Other areas have changed beyond recognition.

This all gives rise to a bunch of interesting spectres and folklore – a large proportion of which are connected to stately houses or castles.

Arthur's Seat.

Seventeen tiny coffins, with carved dolls inside, were found by children in 1836. Their purpose had never been ascertained though it is possible they were put there in sympathy for the victims of Burke and Hare.

Nicol Muschat famously murdered his wife on the slopes in 1720 and was hanged for the offence. Plague victims were housed and buried here. Salisbury crags, which are adjacent, are a favourite spot for suicides.

Barony Street.

The 'Witches Howff' – a suspected coven – was located in a house here in the 17th century. The unfortunate women who lived in it were burned alive

Picardy Place, Top of Leith Walk.

A place of execution where Major Thomas Weir among others, met their end. Picardy Place is also the birthplace of Sir Arthur Conan Doyle – creator of Sherlock Holmes and the man who popularized the Spiritualist movement in Scotland

No 5 Hazeldean Terrace.

In 1957 the Hazeldean Poltergeist became a national phenomenon. By a spectacular coincidence (or perhaps a more sinister reason) it made an appearance at almost the same time and the same house number as the Rothesay Place Poltergeist. In this house a wooden chopping board was frequently propelled across the room, mugs and cups broke in two and the family were kept awake by unexplained banging noises coming from the kitchen. Like the Rothesay Place poltergeist the sightings tailed off after a couple of years.

Edinburgh Playhouse, Greenside Place.

Haunted by Albert, a man in a grey coat, whose appearances on level six are accompanied by a cold spot. He is reputed to be either a stagehand who died in an accident or a night watchman who committed suicide.

Greenside Place was also the site of the Gallow Lee – the public scaffold.

Calton Hill Top of Leith Walk.

Site of Calton jail where executions took place. 17th century lore tells of a gateway here to the fairy kingdom - but only those with second sight could see it. A character called the Fairy boy of Leith acted as the drummer to the elves and fairies who met there every week. The story was made famous in Richard Bovet's book, *Pandæmonium, or the Devil's Cloister Opened.*

South Leith Church, Leith.

This area was where the victims of the 1645 bubonic plague were housed and then buried. One half of the population of Leith died within eight months.

Royal Lyceum Theatre, Lothian Road.

A shadowy figure is sometimes seen perched high in the lighting rig. There are occasional sightings of a blue lady rumoured to be the stage actress Ellen Terry whose first performance, in 1856, was at the Lyceum's opening.

Gillespie Crescent, Bruntsfied.

The site of *Wrychtishousis*, a famous haunted house that has long been demolished. In the 18th century the house, occupied by General Robertson of Lawers, was haunted by a headless woman carrying a child. Though this seems a rather stereotypical spectre, there seemed to be a logical reason for the woman's lack of head. The house had once belonged to a James Clerk, his wife and child. Clerk had died overseas and his younger brother killed the wife and child so that he would inherit the estate. He hid the bodies in a chest but the woman was too large and he had to cut her head off to fit her inside.

This unlikely story seems to have actually been true. When the house was finally knocked down, workmen found a hidden cellar containing the bodies of a child, a woman with a severed head and a confession note from the brother.

Bruntsfield Links.

This triangle of parkland was part of a wasteland called the *Burgh Muir* where armed citizens trained and criminals were executed. In the 16th century plague victims were contained and buried here. There were also burials in the Meadows, the park next to it.

Leamington Terrace, Bruntsfield.

Residents in the street insist there is some kind of supernatural 'presence' here – although no physical manifestation of this has ever been recorded.

No 21 Spottiswood Street, Marchmont

Site of the Marchmont Chaperone, a demonic entity who appeared briefly in 1987.

The Grange Cemetery, Marchmont.

Burial Place of Hugh Millar the famous Victorian palaeontologist, geologist and writer who lived in Edinburgh and Portobello. Despite his eminence as a scientist Millar claimed to have several supernatural encounters. Claiming to be haunted by supernatural visions, he shot himself in 1856. He was buried on the same day as a firearms expert, Thomas Leslie. Despite 25 years experience, Leslie managed to accidentally kill himself with Millar's gun right after Millar did.

Balcarres Street, Morningside.

Haunted by a green lady. The spectre is reputed to be Elizabeth Pittendale – married to Sir Thomas Elphinstone in the early 18th century. She was caught by her husband in a passionate embrace with his own son by a former marriage – a gentleman with the rather sexy name of Jack Courage. Sir Thomas stabbed his wife to death and then committed suicide. When Jack Courage died, Elizabeth's coffin was moved from her husband's plot to his and the apparition was never seen again.

Gilmerton Grange.

The area where this small farmhouse stood is haunted by Margaret Herring who lived in the area in the 14th century. Her father, Sir John Herring, demanded she stop meeting her lover there - but she defied him. He burned the building to the ground with his daughter inside. Her last recorded sighting was in 1960.

Edinburgh Festival Theatre, Nicholson Street.

Standing on the site of the old *Empire Palace*, the Festival Theatre is haunted by a tall dark stranger, who may be the famous illusionist Sigmund Neuberger, the *Great Lafayette*. Lafayette was playing the Empire Palace in 1911 when the stage caught fire – and one of his props was a live lion who was trapped backstage. Lafayette ran back to shoot the beast (presumably shouting "You can't leave that lion there!") and was burned to death, along with nine stagehands. By a macabre twist his identically dressed stage double was also killed – so maybe *that's* who haunts the Festival Theatre.

Dalry Road.

Once haunted by Johnny 'One-Arm' Chiesly. In 1689 he shot the Lord President of the Court of Session, Sir George Lockhart of Carnworth, because Carnworth had awarded Chiesly's wife a large divorce settlement. The hand that pulled the trigger was cut off before he was hanged and his corpse was stolen from the gallows. Some people have no luck.

Johnny hasn't been seen since 1965 when a skeleton, missing its right hand was discovered under the hearthstones of a Dalry cottage that had just been demolished.

47 Stevenson Drive, Stenhouse.

Occupied by a Mrs Rodgers until her death in 1954. Not long after, undecipherable writing appeared on the wall of the house. Her husband claimed his wife was attempting to contact him. Frustratingly for his deceased partner, he never did work out what she was trying to tell him and the writing eventually ceased.

The Manse, Colinton.

A pale, long haired spirit can sometimes be seen hiding behind a yew tree in the garden. It was written about by Robert Louis Stevenson, whose grandfather's house was next door.

The Corn Exchange, Baltic street.

Haunted by a 19th century Leith publican who allegedly tortured children. Shunned by his neighbours, he hanged himself in an upstairs room. His victims can also be heard crying there. One of the few spooks in Edinburgh supposedly captured on camera, it featured on the American TV series *Understanding the Paranormal*.

The Dovecot, Dovecot Road, Corstorphine.

The patch of garden around the dovecot is haunted by Christian Nimmo, the White Lady of Corstorphine, who sometimes carries a sword. Nimmo was the feisty young wife of a prosperous merchant and in love with James Baillie Forrester of Corstorphine castle. When her lover, who had a bit of a drink problem, insulted her, she stabbed him to death. Despite claiming to be pregnant with his child, then escaping from prison dressed as a man, she was beheaded in 1679.

This has given rise to another legend – the *Curse of the Dovecot.* If the eponymous three story building, all that is left of Corstorphine castle, is ever demolished the lady of the house will die within the year.

Craigcrook Castle, Corstorphine Hill.

Haunted by the ghost of the writer and Lord Advocate, Lord Francis Jeffrey, who lived there until his death in 1850. There are cold spots, small objects moving, phantom footsteps and a doorbell that rings when nobody is near it.

Lauriston Castle.

There was once an aged and infirm manservant employed there and he used to shuffle around the castle in his slippers. Now the sound of phantom footsteps are often heard moving quickly through the building. Whether they are heading in the direction of the nearest toilet has never been ascertained.

Barnbougle Castle, Cramond.

Haunted by the Hound of Barnbougle, which howls at nearby Hound Point each time a laird of the castle dies. The original animal was taken to the crusades by its master Roger De Mowbray, who died in Syria on the Crusades. The haunting is commemorated in the lines of an old ballad

And ever when Barnbougle's lords

Are parting this scene below
Come hound and ghost to this haunted coast
With death notes winding slow.

Caroline Park House (also known as Royston House), Granton.
Haunted by a Green Lady believed to be the wife of the one-time owner, Sir James Mackenzie. She appears through a wall at midnight and passes the main entrance before disappearing. She then pops up again in the east courtyard where she rings an old bell. The house is unusual in that it has a phantom cannonball. Twice in the 19th century it flew in a window, came to a stop and then vanished – both incidents were witnessed by Lady John Scott, who wrote *Annie Laurie*. A loud unexplained banging has also been heard coming from one particular room – but let's not speculate on that.

Muirhouse Gardens.
A more modern haunting, since these low rise flats were only built in the mid-20th century. An old man with long tangled hair and blank eyes flits from tree to tree along the street. The trees are far older than the surrounding buildings.

Cheyne Street, Stockbridge.
Home of Jessie King, the 'Stockbridge Baby Farmer'. In the 18th century she took in orphans for payment and then murdered them. She was hanged in 1889.

Pinkie House.
The wife of the first Earl of Dunfermline appears whenever a misfortune is about to befall the Drummond family, owners of the house.

Craigcrook Castle.
An invisible entity throws small objects like paperclips and screws around.

Borthwick Castle, Gorebridge.

Now a hotel, its Red Room is haunted by a young girl known as Anne Grant. She was supposedly a peasant's daughter who was made pregnant by Lord Borthwick. To prevent the complications of an illegitimate heir he then murdered the girl. Despite being exorcised she still slams doors shut on men's fingers. Understandably she has a dislike of males.

Crichton Castle, Midlothian.

Haunted by a figure on horseback who rides through the castle wall. It is thought to be Sir William Crichton, Chancellor of Scotland in the 15th century. It was he who organized the 'Black Dinner' in 1440 at Edinburgh Castle. The Earl of Douglas and his brother, both children, were invited to the castle to dine with the boy king James III. Since they were contenders to the throne they were murdered when they arrived.

Dalhousie Castle, Lasswade.

Haunted by a Grey Lady who is seen in the dungeons and the stairwell. She is thought to be a mistress of one of the Lairds who was lured to the castle by his jealous wife. Once inside she was locked up and starved to death. By coincidence, the castle was once occupied by Sir Alexander Ramsey, Earl of Dalhousie. Imprisoned by Sir William Douglas in 1342, Ramsey starved to death – though he managed to last 17 days because small amounts of grain fell into his dungeon from the granary above.

Presumably one starving ghost is enough at Dalhousie so Ramsay haunts Hermitage Castle instead.

Hunter's Tryst Inn, Oxgangs.

Haunted by a White Lady. Yup. Another one.

Mount Lothian Quarry, Penicuik.

Haunted by a galloping horseman. In the late 19th century a young farm labourer 'borrowed' a horse from his master to visit a young lady. Passing the quarry he came across an upturned cart with the driver trapped underneath. Whether he was frightened that his theft would be discovered or simply very callous, the young man rode by without giving aid.

The driver later died, but not before telling local rescuers how he had been treated. The locals were horrified by the young man's actions and he lost his job, his girlfriends and his self-respect. Not long after he was found dead, possibly by suicide – though its more likely he was killed by friends of the cart driver. He was buried in unconsecrated ground.

Roslin.

Haunted by Lady Bothwell – though she hasn't been seen for half a century. 20th Century sightings include the Mauthe Hound, the ghost of an apprentice and the Black Cannons. Also reputed to be the site where the Holy Grail is buried.

The A7.

Haunted by, of all things, a phantom lorry. It drives along the Gala Water section and is blamed for causing a number of accidents on that particular road.

The B1348.

Not to be outdone by some 'A' road, this thoroughfare is travelled by a phantom bus, which seems to be a ghostly shuttle between Prestonpans and Cockenzie.

Acknowledgements

Adams, Norman, *Haunted Scotland* (Mainstream, Edinburgh 1998)

Ansdell Ian, *Strange Tales of Edinburgh* (Lang Syne, Edinburgh 1975)

Baigent, Michael, Leigh, Richard and Lincoln, Henry, *The Messianic Legacy* (New York: Henry Holt, 1986),

Baily, Helen, *My Love affair with Borthwick Castle* (Book guild 1988)

Bardens, Dennis, *Ghosts and Hauntings* (Zeuss Press 1965)

Beaumont, William Comyns, (1947) *Britain the Key to World History* (Rider & Co London 1947)

Chambers, Robert, *Traditions of Edinburgh* (London 1824)

Cohen, Daniel, *Encyclopaedia of Ghosts* (Michael O Mara Books 1984)

Coventry, Martin, *The Haunted Castles of Scotland* (Goblinshead 1999)

Fife, Malcolm, *The Nor Loch*, (Pentland Press, Edinburgh 2001)

Grant, James, *Cassell's Old And New Edinburgh*. (London 1880)

Green, Andrew, *Haunted Houses* (Shire 1975)

Halliday, Ron, *Paranormal Scotland* (Black and White, Edinburgh 2000)

Henderson, Jan-Andrew, *The Town Below the Ground* (Mainstream, Edinburgh 1999) - *The Emperor's New Kilt* (Mainstream Edinburgh 2000)

- *The Ghost That Haunted Itself* (Mainstream, Edinburgh 2001)

- *Secret City* (OUP, Oxford 2004)

Lennon John and Foley Malcolm, *Dark Tourism: The Attraction of Death and Disaster* (Continuum 2000)

Love, Diane, *Scottish Ghosts* (Robert Hale, London 1995)

- *Scottish Spectres* (Robert Hale, London 2001)

Matthews, Rupert, *Haunted Edinburgh* (Pitkin 1993)

Mitchell, Robin, *Adam Lyal's Witchery Tales* (Cadies, Edinburgh 1988)

O Donnell, Elliot, *Scottish Ghost Stories* (London 1895)

Partner, Peter *The Murdered Magicians: The Templars and Their Myth* (New York: Oxford University Press. 1982),

Richardson, Robert *The Unknown Treasure: The Priory of Sion Fraud and the Spiritual Treasure of Rennes-le-Château* (Houston, TX: North Star, 1998)

Robertson, *James Scottish Ghost Stories* (Warner, London 1996)

- *The Fanatic* (Harper Collins London 2000)

Scott, Walter, *Minstrelsy of the Scottish Border* (Singing Tree Press, Detroit 1968)

Sinclair George, *Satan's Invisible World Discovered* (Edinburgh 1685)

Stein, Walter Johannes *The Ninth Century: World History in the Light of the Holy Grail* (London: Temple Lodge Press, 1991).

Stevenson, David, *The Beggar's Benison: Sex clubs of Enlightenment Scotland and their Rituals* (Tuckwell Press 2001)

Thomson, Francis, *Ghosts Sprits and Spectres of Scotland* (Impulse 1973)

Turnbull, Michael, *Edinburgh Characters* (St Andrew 1992)

Underwood Peter, *Gazetteer of Scottish Ghosts* (London 1974)

Wallace-Murphy, Tim, *An Illustrated Guide To Roslin Chapel* (Roslin 1993)

Watt, Francis, *The Book of Edinburgh Anecdotes* (London 1913)

Wiseman, Richard. Watt, Caroline. Stevens, Paul. Greening, Emma. O Keeffe, Ciaran, *An investigation into alleged 'hauntings'* (British Journal of Psychology 2003 94, 195-211)

Woodrow, Robert, *Materials for a History of Remarkable Providences; mostly relating to Scotch Ministers and Christians* (Edinburgh 1843)

In the course of my research I have referred to local guidebooks, newspaper and television reports, web sites and eyewitness accounts. My thanks to everyone I interviewed or talked to, or who sent or emailed me stories. Additional material was provided by *The Edinburgh Evening News, The Scotsman, The Scottish Sun, The Daily Record, News of the World, The Guardian, The Sunday Herald, UK Paranormal, Mystery Hunters, Readers Digest, Most Haunted, Jane Goldman Investigates, Unexplained, The Fortean Times, Beyond Chance, The World's Scariest Places Firstfoot.com, Auld Reekie Tours, The Real Mary King's Close, The Witchery Tours and Edinburgh University Parapsychology Department.*

ABOUT THE AUTHOR

Jan-Andrew (J A) Henderson is the author of 25 fiction and non-fiction books and winner of the Royal Mail and Doncaster Book Awards. He also owns City of the Dead Ghost Tours.

www.cityofthedeadtours.com

His non-fiction includes

The Town Below the Ground: Edinburgh's Underground City
The Ghost that Haunted Itself: The Story of Mackenzie Poltergeist
The Emperor's New Kilt: The Two Secret Histories of Scotland
Black Markers: Edinburgh's History Told Through Its Graveyards
The Old Town: A Comprehensive Guide
The New Town: A Comprehensive Guide

For regular **free** books, stories, news and advice, subscribe to his website at www.janandrewhenderson.com

CPSIA information can be obtained
at www.ICGtesting.com
Printed in the USA
BVHW031058120121
597628BV00008B/146